My Dear Watson

Penny Watson

My Dear Watson

The Story of a Football Marriage

Arthur Barker Limited London
A subsidiary of Weidenfeld (Publishers) Limited

Published in Great Britain by
Arthur Barker Ltd
91 Clapham High Street
London SW4 7TA

ISBN 0 213 16814 6

Printed in Great Britain by
Butler & Tanner Ltd
Frome and London

Contents

Illustrations

To David.

I could not have written it without him.

Preface

When I first decided to attempt to write this book, I intended it to be concerned mainly with football, from a wife's point of view. Inevitably, however, it has also resulted in a sort of informal biography of my husband's career. That is hardly surprising, though, when our lives are so intertwined. Most of the relevant facts are included, and to the best of my knowledge they are accurate. After sifting through his dozen or so scrap-books and many football programmes, I have tried to ensure, for those interested in statistics, that the most important of these appear in the following text.

It has been difficult at times to find the strength and energy to put words on paper. Mostly, though, it has been frustrating not having enough hours in the day to divide my time between mother, wife and writer and to still find some enthusiasm for leisure activities. My biggest problem in life has always been my sometimes explosive impatience and sense of urgency to get things done 'yesterday'. As soon as I have conceived an idea pertaining to the book, I have been eager to see that idea in writing, but unfortunately time has not always permitted that and then frustration has set in. At times I thought I would never be able to complete my book, but thankfully I have. I hope that those who read it will think my effort was worth while.

1

On the Dole

Notts County, 1967

The public's image of a footballer's life is one of glamour and excitement, and many people would love to be involved in the profession. However, only those actually in the game, those who have actually experienced life in football, can know the reality. Do not misunderstand, it is not a bad life, in fact most of the time it is very good if one is prepared to be separated from one's spouse for long periods of time. Sometimes, however, it can be hell, with football seeming like a demanding mistress pulling the player away from his family, constantly seeking his attention and always receiving precedence. Contrary to public opinion footballers in general are not highly paid and many do have to resort to the dole queue when they finally hang up their boots, because a football career is so very short and most players do not earn enough money during their playing lives to continue to support a family afterwards. Too many youngsters go into the game at a tender age without any qualifications or abilities to fall back on when their playing days are over – hence the dole queue. I often wonder how many players stay in soccer, as coaches for example, because they really want to, and how many because there are no other options open to them.

Thankfully I am not in such a precarious position, because my husband, as well as being a highly talented player, has been fortunate, worked hard and looked to the future. Over the years, though, I have seen many who do fall into the above category.

Being married to a professional footballer is not drastically different from being married to anyone else; I still have to do the same dreary things all housewives have to do. However, I have been places I might never have seen, met people I most certainly would not have met and enjoyed a lifestyle I doubt very much that I would otherwise have achieved. They are all due to my husband's success. Because there is no doubt about it: Dave Watson is a success. He may not have the public image of Kenny Dalglish, nor the money of Kevin Keegan, but ask anyone in football and they would agree that in his own right he is a success.

When I first met Dave, over thirteen years ago in May 1967, I had no way of knowing that the tall, very quiet, not very stylish young man stood in front of me was destined to be known all over Europe, and that ultimately I would share my life with a truly famous person.

Indeed in the beginning I did not even particularly like what I saw. I was still very young, only sixteen, and I already had a steady boyfriend. I only danced with Dave that night in 'The Beachcomber', Nottingham, because my friend, Helen, was potty about Dave's friend, John Wright. It took Dave three months of persistence before I finally gave in and went out with him. The date was 20 August 1967, and from that day on there has only been one man for me.

When I first knew him he was painfully shy and would blush at the slightest thing. He's changed a lot since then! At our first meeting he told me that he worked in the wholesale fruit and vegetable market in Nottingham, and never mentioned anything about football. It was true that at that time he was working at the market, because it was the close season in football and he had to get a summer job to supplement his meagre take-home pay of ten pounds a week, and it did help to while away the long summer break that footballers used to get in those days. In the sixties only top-flight clubs went on tours, and Notts County were still in the Fourth Division. Dave had signed professional forms only a few months before meeting me, and he was already twenty – quite old for a footballer to be taking his first tentative steps towards stardom. This just goes to show that you do not have to enter football very young and sign schoolboy forms with a club to become successful. So is the great wastage really necessary? Would the very few who come through the system to success not have made the grade anyway, without committing themselves totally at such an early age? I personally feel that the end does not justify the means in this case, because too many youngsters have to face life as a 'failure' at a very early age when they are rejected by a club, and of the few who do go right through only a handful will have earned enough to cope financially after their playing career is over. Thankfully though some clubs are now aware of this dilemma and do encourage youngsters to continue their educational studies and apprenticeships in conjunction with their football, before concentrating solely on the game. This gives them something to fall back on if they fail to make it in football, or whenever their careers come to an end.

David's somewhat belated entry into League football is worth elaborating. At the age of fifteen he left his local secondary school and went into farming as a labourer. It is not surprising that he had not passed his eleven plus examination to go on to grammar school in the footsteps of some of the rest of his family, because at Dave's junior school he had been encouraged to miss lessons to play football. The games master often interrupted a scheduled lesson to ask for Dave's help on the sports field! The idea of this happening today is inconceivable, but nevertheless it did happen. Fortunately Dave was to make use of those extra football lessons in later life, but had he not have entered into a career in football he would have been found sadly lacking in some of the basic academic skills thanks to that all-important first school not fulfilling its responsibilities.

Later on David loved the open-air life on the dairy farm where he worked. He has always had an affinity with animals and had kept quite a strange menagerie, his mother permitting, in their back garden, so working with the cows found him in his element. The only part of his work that he had really hated was seeing the calves being taken to slaughter. That really upset him, and even to this day he will not eat veal.

After a year of farm life, his family persuaded him that his job had no prospects for him and the long hours and low pay could be bettered in another career. So David then commenced an apprenticeship as an electrician with a local firm. He served three years with them but was then made redundant on account of the company's financial difficulties. Unable to find another position, he was forced to draw unemployment benefit. Like most people who have to queue up in those depressing places, Dave felt humiliated and demoralized when he went to collect his 'dole' money each week.

Fortunately there was the alternative of football. In his early school days he had played football during almost every waking hour and had captained his school teams. From school he went on to local boys' clubs and represented Nottinghamshire in two youth league games.

Looking back, it is obvious that Dave's four elder brothers must have had a great deal of influence upon his football development when he was still quite young. They had all had connections with football at some level or other.

Dave's second eldest brother, Peter, was a professional footballer with Nottingham Forest and Southend United and often used to play football in the back garden of the family's council home, teaching the young David to head the ball properly. Peter had been a promising centre-half, but a serious injury eventually forced him out of the game prematurely. The eldest brother, Tony, was a keen amateur footballer and at one time was the manager of the local semi-professional non-League side, Long Eaton. Fred, who is six years older than David, played for the police while he was in the force, and Jack, the 'brainy' one of the family with an M.Sc., played in several university games.

It was Tony who had persuaded Dave to go for a trial at Notts County. I think Tony knew somebody down at Meadow Lane, where arrangements were made for Dave's test. County must have been interested as they signed him immediately, though only on amateur forms at first; obviously they did not want to stick their necks out and sign him professionally until he had proved himself. In time Dave signed professional forms and made his League debut against Chester on 28 March 1967. He received promising reports afterwards, but he had only made his way into the first team on account of an injury to the first-choice left-back, Terry Thompson, and for the following game he was dropped because Thompson had recovered.

Over the next few months Dave was in and out of the team. He played a total of eight positions for County and the manager, Billy Gray, was once quoted as saying, 'For me [Dave] had always got to be in my team in some position – he was that good a player.' Actually Billy Gray preferred to play him as centre-forward, explaining, 'I had him at centre-forward for the simple reason that we had a solid and recognized Number Five but lacked strength up front. He had such good ball control, excellent timing and heading ability that he was a natural for the role of striker.' In those days Dave was just happy to be playing League football in any position. He could not believe his luck in actually being paid for something he loved doing. He was keen to improve his developing skills and would often return in the afternoon to do some extra training and to receive special coaching from David Coates. Coatsie taught Dave a great deal, and whenever Dave is asked to whom he owes a lot in football, he always says David Coates.

It was during those tentative early months in professional football that we met. I cannot recall a great deal of those early days with regard to football. I only managed to visit Meadow Lane a couple of times, as I had a Saturday job, but my parents both charted Dave's progress carefully as they were ardent football fans and supported Notts County. (They had a couple of season tickets in the stand at that time, but for many years previously had stood amongst the crowds on the terraces at Notts County one week, then at Nottingham Forest the next.) I had always been 'sporty' and enjoyed watching football. Hardly surprising, when you consider the environment I grew up in. However, I had never been able to attend matches myself as I was training as a dancer and almost all my free time was taken up with that.

Two or three evenings each week after school, and almost all day Saturday, I would be found at Miss Tozer's dance studio. I had taken up dancing when I was young following medical advice. My legs had been badly bowed, and the local clinic had wanted to put me into callipers to help straighten them. My own doctor, however, fearing I may become dependent on the contraptions, advised my parents to send me to ballet classes as this would help strengthen and straighten my legs. I suppose physiotherapy was not as readily available then as it is now, and that dancing was the next best thing. The dancing 'bug' bit, and I used to travel all over the country entering competitions and dance festivals in all aspects of stage dance, including tap, greek, acrobatics and different styles of ballet. The dance school I attended also gave drama lessons. These I adored, and at one time I had aspired to attending RADA but sadly that never materialized and eventually I gave up most of my dancing too, as I decided that I did not want to go on to the stage as a professional dancer. My GCE exams were imminent and the dancing was taking up a lot of my time so I chose to concentrate on my school work. Then I met Dave. However, the years of dancing lessons were not entirely a waste of time or money, because my legs are perfectly straight now, and also, because of my own dancing, my brother entered the profession to become one of the best male stage dancers in the business.

One of the first games I went to watch at Notts County with my parents was to prove to be one of Dave's most memorable matches. It was against Crewe Alexandra, and played on 4 October 1967, the eve of his twenty-first birthday. Dave's family had not arranged any celebrations for him (he was the youngest of eight children, and there had never been much money around for parties), so my father had organized a small dinner party for Dave at a plush Nottingham hotel after the game. David made the evening complete by scoring his first League goal that night. He said very little at the celebration. He seemed pre-occupied, and was obviously reliving his first important goal over and over again in his mind. I think that was the moment when I realized what an important part of Dave's life football was, and even though we had been courting for only a couple of months I hoped that I would be allowed to share that life with him.

Only four months after Dave and I had started going out together Notts County decided that David was superfluous to their needs. When an offer came in for him from Rotherham United manager Tommy Docherty, Dave was sold to the Yorkshire club. Billy Gray said that it was for Dave's own benefit that he agreed to the transfer to Rotherham. He knew Tommy Docherty would give Dave that extra shot of confidence he lacked at that stage of his development. So Dave moved on to play football in a higher division and was never to look back.

Dave:

When I look back to my early football at Notts County, all I remember is total enjoyment. Being paid to play football was a dream come true for me. During that period I made several friends and learned a lot about professional football. In a sense, I was a minor celebrity. From being an out of work electrician, a nobody, I was a pro footballer – on the way up, I hoped.

One of the players I made friends with was also a coach, David Coates. I think that much of my early encouragement came from David and I realize I owe a great deal to him.

After seeing Penny for the first time, I liked what I saw, so I tried to make an impression on her – unfortunately without much success at first. However, after quite a long period I managed to win her heart and I believe I have kept it ever since. Our relationship blossomed very quickly, but just when we were really getting to know each other, I moved to Rotherham.

2

Wedding Bells

Rotherham United, 1967-70

Only a month after Tommy Docherty himself joined Rotherham, who were then struggling at the bottom of the Second Division, he bought an unknown player from the Fourth Division to help his team stave off the threat of relegation. Dave was exuberant, of course, but the sad thing was that just as our courtship was taking shape Dave had to go and live in another town, which meant we could no longer see each other almost every day, as we had been used to. Dave used to collect me from college in his A35 van, which co-incidentally he bought the day he started going out with me, and we would go out with each other most evenings. Transferring to Rotherham Dave had to go into 'digs' – something that was completely alien to him, as he is a very homely person and does not take kindly to change in his home life. I remember going with him to sign for Rotherham. Yes, he took me along – though I did not even get out of the car – but, stranger still, he took his mother too! Looking back, it would have seemed very odd to any onlooker: a grown man of twenty-one taking his mother with him. Fortunately the other players had the day off and nobody saw her, so Dave was saved the inevitable ragging he would otherwise have received.

Initially the club arranged digs for him, but these proved to be unsuitable. Fortunately Dave's brother, Fred, lived in a place called Worksop, where he was serving in the police force, and as Worksop is within reasonable travelling distance of Rotherham Dave stayed there. By now it had become apparent that Dave and I were in love, and on the anniversary of our first date we became engaged. We had a party at my parents' home and in addition to our family and friends, some of the Rotherham players, together with Tommy Docherty and his wife Agnes, came to help the celebrations along. Dave was in some discomfort that night, though, as he had broken one of his ribs in the game that day (any excuse to avoid dancing!).

Even though Tommy Docherty's young team fought a tremendous battle to avoid relegation, their revival was not enough and sadly at the end of the 1967–68 season they went down into the Third Division. However, one great consolation to the players that season was their terrific run in the FA Cup. They received the *Sunday Mirror* 'Giant Killers Cup' taking First Division Leicester City to a replay and only losing in extra time, after temporarily halting their march to a place in the final eight.

Dave was an immediate success at Rotherham and the fans took to him instantly. Tommy Docherty's faith in David certainly paid off, and the new techniques he was taught under the Doc's watchful eye gradually gave him the confidence he had hitherto been lacking. We felt grateful to the Doc for this, although we were less keen on some of the regulations he tried to enforce. One of the more curious ones was that the players were not to have sex after a Wednesday, before a Saturday game. Even now some rather old-fashioned managers believe in this regime. It is rather ridiculous when one remembers how hard footballers train and what fit athletes players should be. In those days it was considered that love-making was equivalent to a five-mile run. This theory has now been totally disproved by medical research, but nevertheless some managers of the 'old school' still hold fast to this ruling. Another thing that has changed greatly over the years is the diet of a footballer before a game. Pre-match meals in the sixties invariably consisted of steak or poached eggs. Medical science has proved since that the proteins and fats contained in those foods take longer to digest than carbohydrates. More players now eat things like cornflakes or toast and honey before a game, so that there is time for the food to be completely digested before they start running around. There are still one or two traditionalists who religiously eat their steaks, regardless of the fact that most of it will still be in their stomachs when the kick-off whistle is blown.

After staying with his brother for about eighteen months Dave moved in with Jim Furnell and his wife Pam, who also lived near Worksop. (Jim was then the goalkeeper with Rotherham United.) Fred's wife Brenda had given birth to their third child, and their small home was beginning to become overcrowded. While staying with the Furnells, David was able to keep his eye on the progress of our first home, which was being built on the same estate as Jim's house. We planned to be married in June 1969. That meant that I would still be eighteen, but we knew that we could either be married then or else would have to wait another year until the end of the following season. (Neither of us wanted to tie the knot during the season, for that would have meant that we would not be able to have a proper honeymoon. Some players do marry in the season, but I personally cannot understand this.) Dave and I were separated by his job. We wanted to be together, so the best solution was to be married straight away.

Twelve months after coming to Rotherham, Tommy Docherty shocked everyone at Millmoor by moving to manage Queens Park Rangers. Months before this he had had to stave off several inquiries to buy David, who had swiftly become one of the club's most valuable assets. Clubs, who were reputed to have been watching Dave closely were Nottingham Forest, Everton, Liverpool, Manchester United, Birmingham, West Bromwich Albion and Coventry City. It was reported that Docherty had refused three huge offers. In order to dampen these clubs' enthusiasm Tommy Docherty put an inflated price tag of £90,000 upon David. However, when the Doc left the club the papers reported that he was interested in purchasing Dave himself, but that Queens Park Rangers funds could not approach that estimate!

Tommy Docherty had accumulated a youthful team, which was inherited by Jim McAnearney, the new manager. The Doc has always been able to do his best work with younger players and Dave had really enjoyed his coaching methods, which were refreshing, if sometimes pretty gruelling. Everyone was a little surprised and very sad when he did leave for the London club.

Jim McAnearney took over as manager and if one was to believe the numerous articles that constantly appeared in the Press, David was still being watched by every top-class club in the country. In fact the clubs that were *not* reported as being interested in Dave were not worth mentioning! Leicester City, Arsenal, Leeds, Spurs and Newcastle United were all added to the list. Perhaps there was some truth in these rumours. I would like to think so, but unfortunately a lot may have been the product of the imagination of some reporter, anxious to fill space in his sports column. Quite often what happens is that the manager of a top-class club watches a game and before he knows it he is reported as 'checking up' on a specific player with the intention of buying that player. The reporters probably think there is little harm in their conjectures, but reports like this can be very unsettling. Indeed they did prompt Dave, who was curious to know whether there was any substance in the reports, to wonder if he might genuinely have First Division potential. This curiosity resulted in a transfer request which was quickly refused by the manager and directors at Rotherham.

Our wedding on 21 June 1969, at St Peter's Church in the Nottinghamshire village of Ruddington, was a very special day for me – as every wedding is to a bride! Dave was not a big football star at that time, so we were able to have a normal wedding without the circus that there would have been if we had waited a few years and married when he was famous. Many people who know us both say that if Dave had not married me he probably would not have become so successful. I really do not know about that, but it is true that he did need a push in the early days in almost everything he did, and I had to coax him quite a lot. In the first few years he would never make an important decision without hearing my suggestions, and while I agree that in a marriage that is good to a certain extent, in retrospect I think that he did rely on me too much. The fact that he was born under the star of Libra has, no doubt, something to do with his incessant procrastination and indecision. Thankfully he is very much his own master now, and it has given me a sense of relief to know that I do not have to take so much responsibility for decision-making. We have always been a unit which has functioned best when we are together, and apart from anything else we have been good friends. This has forged a bond between us and given our marriage a special quality that some other marriages lack. Of course we do have our moments of disagreement, but I believe that this is healthy, natural and extremely necessary for a marriage to survive the pressures of modern-day living.

Jimmy McAnearney and his wife, along with a few of the Rotherham players, attended the wedding, which on

Dave's insistence was a 'top hat and tails' ceremony. I must admit that they all looked very smart in their morning dress and David really looked a million dollars in his light grey suit. His best man was a friend of ours called Gren, and his fiancée, Carole, was a bridesmaid. They had been our closest friends during our courtship and we went almost everywhere in a foursome. My friend, Fiona, was the chief bridesmaid of four, and there were two page boys. Fiona and I had gone to school together, and our friendship has lasted even to this day. We used to argue a great deal in our schooldays, but there must be something that has kept us friends all these years. Fiona is a funny girl, in the nicest sense of the word. For example, when she was younger and a boy would ask her what her father did, she would say that he was in the building trade. In actual fact her father is a director of Wimpeys, the builders.

Rather sad absentees from the festivities were Jim and Pam Furnell. Dave and I were rather worried when they did not arrive, for we knew that they were coming and that Jim had even hired his morning suit. We found out later that they were on their way, Jim dressed up, and their car broke down en route from Carlton-in-Lindrick to Ruddington. A rather embarrassed Jim had to take the car to the nearest garage, complete with top hat and tails.

After our honeymoon, which we had spent at Salou in Spain, we returned to our new home, in Carlton-in-Lindrick, where Dave carried me over the threshold. David has never, outwardly, been a romantic or passionate individual. I believe he feels that showing one's emotions is a sign of weakness, but even he can surpass himself on occasions and I was very touched when he transported me in the age-old traditional way without any prompting from me. Carlton-in-Lindrick is a small village just north of Worksop which is right in the heart of Sherwood Forest country, and we would make many excursions into Clumber Park to visit the undulating grounds in search of wildlife and romp through the woods with Dave's alsatian dog, Ranje.

Our little bungalow, which was detached and had three bedrooms, seemed like a palace to us, and was a very good start for any newly married couple. The walls were paper thin, and the quality of the building was poor, but nevertheless it was our haven and we both loved it. Dave worked hard inside and out and, with the help of his Rotherham colleague and room mate Dave Bentley, built a cupboard and bookshelves in the lounge. However, with all their clowning around, I think it took them twice as long to complete than it should have, and the finished article was not quite perpendicular to the wall. Nevertheless they had tried! The two Daves were good friends and had shared many amusing moments.

One such episode which must be related, even though Dave swears he had nothing to do with it, occurred when Rotherham were visiting Plymouth. The team had won and the victors decided to celebrate before travelling home to the north as they were staying the night after the game. David went to bed early, as he has never enjoyed heavy drinking, only to be woken up in the middle of the night by a frantic night porter asking for Dave's assistance in controlling his team-mates. It transpired that several had consumed too much and were by then rather drunk. They had felt hungry and decided to seek nourishment in the kitchens. Opening what they had believed to be a huge refrigerator, they were greeted by the site of succulent roasting ducklings. The refrigerator was in fact an oven containing rows of roasting spits. A couple of the players, who I might add were senior professionals, saw an end to their hunger and with their bare hands seized the ducklings – which were in the process of cooking and therefore very hot. The message that the trays of food were burning them did not reach their beer-soaked brains immediately, but when it did they dropped the birds all over the floor – grease and fat running everywhere. Not to be beaten by this slight problem, they found some telephone directories, placed the ducklings in them, and retreated to devour their prey. The resulting mess, which they apparently had not seen, or which had not registered in their minds, was left for a fretful John Quinn, the skipper, to endeavour, without much success, to clean up. After eating the birds they jettisoned the remains out of their bedroom window on to another guest's car.

Other players had taken possession of the switchboard and were phoning their team-mates who had retired early. Unfortunately they managed to find the wrong rooms at times, and woke up the other irate guests.

The behaviour of the culprits is inexcusable, but when the story is retold it is difficult not to see the funny side. The net result was that the team were banned from that hotel and on future visits to play Plymouth they had to stay in Torquay. The team paid damages, each player contributing around £40, which was a lot of money ten years ago, regardless of whether they were involved or not. Such antics were not uncommon amongst soccer and rugby teams in those days, but the unruly element – which was, I believe, completely without malice – has in the main been eradicated.

Dave worked extremely hard on the garden of our new home. The contractors had left it looking like a building site. On his way to training he passed a market gardeners' and nurseries, and almost every day he came home with different shrubs and plants, and if the weather was fine he would be out in the garden all afternoon.

I had been a shorthand typist for a bank in the local head

offices in Nottingham, where I did personnel work, but when we were married I was forced to transfer to a branch in Worksop, as Nottingham was too far for me to travel to work each day. I did not have my own transport in those days. I found branch work completely different to that which I had enjoyed so much before. My hours were somewhat irregular as no one could leave the bank until all the cashiers had balanced their money and even though I finished my work at the same time each day I never knew what time I would be home. This did not please Dave. He had already had to pacify himself all afternoon, and was usually anxious for me to return home so that we could have our evening meal.

After a couple of months I resigned from my job so that I could be with Dave as much as possible. Most football clubs train each morning for a couple of hours and only go back in the afternoon during pre-season or early season. There is a slight variation on this, of course, but in the main this regime is adhered to. It may seem 'cushy' but remember that it is not uncommon to have to go into work on a Sunday and every bank holiday, including Christmas Day, is a working day for a professional footballer. The more successful the player, the more he is absent from home. With European games, international games and tours, a player could find he has only three or four weeks free in the summer for a holiday, which is not much compensation for all those missed public holidays. However, I suppose that is the price of success in almost every walk of life. The more successful a man becomes, the more he has to be away from home, in the fields of sport, business and many other occupations.

In late September 1969 David again asked for a transfer. We had both wanted him to play in a higher grade of football as it was becoming apparent that he had Second or First Division potential. After a little persuasion from me he wrote out his transfer request, and to his surprise the board at Rotherham granted it. However, the expected rush of big clubs did not materialize – probably owing to the large fee that the club were demanding for Dave's services. His ego a little dented, he was forced to withdraw the request a short while later and settle down to the task in hand, which was to play well for Rotherham United.

Dave had always been a favourite of the Millmoor crowd, and one night there were ructions at the ground when, in a League Cup game against Bolton Wanderers, David was sent off along with Roy Greaves, for allegedly fighting. In my opinion it was a very harsh, unfair decision as Dave was only defending himself from the other player's blows by holding him down by the neck and rendering him helpless. You might think I am biased, but in actual fact I am Dave's worst critic and I am certainly not blinded by my love for him. I am born under the star of Virgo and we Virgoans are perfectionists. We also expect the same high standard of other people, and inevitably I have always demanded the best from David. If David had behaved badly I would have been the first to condemn him. In the referee's opinion Dave was fighting too, and he received his marching orders. He could not believe it, and afterwards said that he wished he *had* hit the player: after all, he was sent off anyway.

Jim Furnell and Dave used to take it in turns to drive to training as we lived only two streets away from each other. Another Rotherham player, Barry Mealand, who lived on the same estate, used to travel with them too.

Seven months after we had moved to Carlton-in-Lindrick, Pam Furnell gave birth to a boy, Stephen. This was a particularly happy event as the Furnells had tried for years to have a baby – without any success. Dave was one of the godfathers. Barry Mealand's wife, Jackie, had a boy while living in that fertile village, and – guess what? – I did too. I remember 17 September 1970 very well, though for all the wrong reasons. I had started my contractions at about three in the morning, and by six David was very concerned, as the intervals between them were only five minutes. In the handbook issued by the hospital it stated that as soon as 'pains' were occurring at intervals of ten minutes or less the patient must be taken to the maternity hospital. Mine were never that far apart! Much to my chagrin Dave rang the hospital – I think he was concerned I might deliver at any moment. Before he could refuse the offer, the anonymous voice on the other end of the telephone told him they would send an ambulance, then put the phone down.

I felt rather silly travelling in the ambulance with Dave driving behind in his car, with the dog in too! After a protracted labour of several hours, during which I was left alone for long spells (husbands were not permitted to sit with their wives even during the early stages of labour in that particular hospital in 1970), a vacuum extraction was diagnosed as necessary. This is a rather archaic form of delivery and, thankfully, not regularly used now. The reason for the difficult birth is still a mystery to me. That particular hospital did not believe in enlightening a patient as to what was happening to her own body, and secrecy surrounded everything.

My stay in Kilton Maternity Hospital was not a happy time. On one occasion the matron had demanded why I was not having private treatment. Pam and Jackie had both seen the consultant obstetrician privately, and the matron had presumed, wrongly, that the football club had paid for this. Evidently she thought the club was funding my confinement and that I was pocketing this money. Another contretemps upset me at a time when I was at my most vulnerable, three or four days after delivery. Roger, my son, because of his rather harrowing entry into the world, had been a mucus baby (this is a term given to a baby who has swallowed a lot of mucus while travelling down the birth canal during delivery). This caused him initially to be a poor eater. It would take him so long to consume his bottle that it was soon time for the next feed, and what he did consume he would vomit back, which was not only worrying but soul-destroying. One day one of the staff midwives decided to feed him so that she could see for herself the problem and check on the vomiting. Just as she was feeding him one of the sisters walked briskly through the ward, and obviously saw the nurse with my baby, though she said nothing at the time. Later, when doing her daily rounds, the matron accused me of being uninterested in my baby and made out that I could not be bothered to feed him myself. The whole episode had been misconstrued, and I was conspicuously scolded like a naughty child in front of the other patients for something I had not done. Mercifully, modern midwives and maternity nurses have more compassion and respect for their patients' feelings. I felt so depressed and bewildered that all I could think of was retreating from that terrible institution into the peaceful, sympathetic sanctuary of my own home as soon as possible. I had been so miserable that I was even driven to telephoning Dave at work – something that I never normally did at Rotherham. He arranged with the local domiciliary midwife that I could have my after-care at home, so on the fifth day I discharged myself from hospital.

At the beginning of the 1970–71 season Dave had been switched to centre-forward by Jim McAnearney, though he still insisted on wearing the Number Five shirt. The first game after Roger entered the world, David scored his first and only League hat trick – such was his elation at being a proud dad!

He has always been a caring father and no task has been too menial for him where the children have been concerned. He has been fortunate in that he has been able to share many experiences with the children that other fathers, with normal working hours, have missed out on. Being home most afternoons has meant he sees almost as much of the children as I do.

However, I hasten to add there are several disadvantages in having a footballing father. The more famous the father, the worse it is for the family. In an average, standard family the father might accompany his children on regular excursions for swimming to the public baths or visits to fairs or perhaps trips to the zoo. A famous dad is reluctant to do any of these things if a large crowd is anticipated because, if he is recognized, there can be little peace for his family. If the player's team lose his children can be ridiculed and ostracized, and even though that may seem harmless it can be very disturbing, especially if the father hits a bad patch and such teasing recurs quite frequently. Even though children below school age might see their father more in the day time than the average dad, there are the numerous nights away from home and the abundant tours that take him away for long periods.

The time I regret most not having a normal routine is at Christmas. For the children, strangely enough, it does not seem to trouble them too much. After all, it is the norm for their father to disappear for training on Christmas morning – they have known no different. However, it is harsh for me, and in some ways all the effort and preparations one normally makes for Christmas seem pointless. I long for the day when we can spend a normal Yuletide and celebrate the New Year as others do. Maybe my expectations will not be realized and I shall be disappointed. Something else I would dearly love is for us to be able to go away on holiday just when we like – perhaps during the winter months –

and not have our holidays dictated by the football curriculum. Of course that is impossible while David is still playing soccer in England, but one day I hope that it will happen.

We had a very friendly unit in Carlton-in-Lindrick, and saw a great deal of the Furnells. Being ten years older than me, Pam became like a big sister. Dave and Jim enjoyed each other's company, though I think it would be difficult for anyone not to be sociable with Jim. Prior to his move to Rotherham he had been the goalkeeper at the Arsenal, and was a very amiable and humorous man.

While we were living in Carlton we held a few parties; as most of the lads at that time were single we were one of the few couples within the club who were able to entertain and have such gatherings. They always seemed to be successful, probably because everyone was on such good amicable terms with each other. There were no jealous undertones amongst the Rotterham lot. Those days were still to come.

Even though we were very happy with our life at that time, I once again persuaded Dave to think about furthering his career. At that time he would, quite frankly, have been content to stagnate at Rotherham till the end of his career, but once his ambitions were aroused he too desired greater things. Again the transfer request was not to be fruitful but at least other clubs were realizing that Dave had aspirations of playing at a higher level and that he would be willing to move on to another club. One might think such indications are not necessary, but there are many players, and particularly players' wives, who would not welcome change. Some women panic at the thought of leaving their home town, families and friends and they can often halt their husbands' careers by being so selfish. Sheffield Wednesday had been after Dave over a period of two months, with Rotherham refusing to lower their price tag.

Then a row broke out in the Press concerning an approach by another club. That club were reported to have leaked to the newspapers that they had put in an offer for David before the letter to Rotherham's directors had arrived at the Yorkshire club. Mr Purshouse, the Rotherham chairman, threatened to report the club to the Football League, but I do not think that actually transpired. Once again the newspapers indicated that clubs were trying to buy Dave, but we had no way of knowing what was fact and what was fantasy. A manager is not obliged to tell a player if other clubs are wishing to buy his services, or if any kind of negotiations are being carried on. It is left to the discretion of the manager as to whether or not one is informed of any developments.

We had reconciled ourselves to settling down to another season at Rotherham when right out of the blue, one Sunday in December, David and I were summoned very mysteriously, and after being sworn to secrecy, to an assignation at a motel on the A1 near Doncaster. There, together with Jim McAnearney, we met Alan Brown, who was the manager of Second Division Sunderland AFC. Bingo – at last! After a short discussion David and Alan Brown went into a private room to talk about Dave's contract. We had been aware that something obscure was happening in the background, but had tried to ignore the implications, in order to soften the blow if once again we were disappointed. This was the big one, though. Sunderland had been trying to buy Dave for some time, but Rotherham had insisted that they would only let one of their best assets go for £100,000. Finally Sunderland had capitulated and made an offer which Rotherham had never really dreamed anyone would come up with. They had never wanted to sell David, but a small club like Rotherham could not let the opportunity of recouping such a tremendous profit on a player slip by. To buy him they had paid out something like £1,000, together with another player, and now they were reluctantly selling him for £99,000 more.

So Dave was the second £100,000 player from the Third Division, and one of only a handful from any division to be given a six-figure price tag. After that meeting all hell was let loose. The Press were at the bungalow wanting photographs of the joyous family, and Roger, who was three months old and normally a co-operative photographer's model, found it all very bewildering and refused to smile.

So, after three very happy years at Rotherham, Dave was a Sunderland player and the happy unit we had in Carlton was to be broken up. Jim was transferred to Plymouth Argyle shortly afterwards, and there is not much further one can go in the opposite direction to Sunderland. We never did have the opportunity to say a proper farewell to all the good friends we had made amongst the players at Rotherham. It is a sad fact, but in football not many lasting friendships are made within the game at player level. Some of the players did visit us occasionally when we first lived in Sunderland, but then those same players were transferred somewhere else further afield. It became more difficult to see each other in the season, and the summer break became occupied with tours. So inevitably the friendships faded.

We were starting out on a new adventure in our lives, one we had both desired and anticipated, and we were full of optimism and excitement at the prospects that lay ahead of us. We thought that from then on life would be plain sailing. How naïve this belief was to turn out to be.

Dave:

When I started going out with Penny I bought an A35 van which had cost me a hundred pounds. It was great having my own wheels, however humble. . . . Penny mentions in the book about me taking her and my mother when I went to sign for Rotherham. Being something of a country bumpkin it seemed quite natural to me at the time, but on reflection it must have appeared strange to an onlooker.

After being a pro footballer for less than a year with Notts County, I was wanted by someone else. I could not believe it. I was extremely excited but also a little scared. I did not even know where Rotherham was, so I looked it up on the map – and it was forty miles from home! At that time forty miles was practically abroad to me. When I first went to see Tommy Docherty he was not at the ground, so I had to go back the following day to sign and train. The training there was the hardest I had ever encountered, and it made me realize that to get to the top you had to train damned hard.

In my Rotherham debut we played Queens Park Rangers at Loftus Road and were beaten 6–0 – not a good start. However, they were after all at the top of the Second Division. I became aware of the fact that I was not as fit as I had thought. In training we used to do a lot of shuttle runs and a sprinting exercise called 'doggies'. This consisted of running between two fixed points – in our case each end of the gym. You would start at one end and sprint to the other end and back again, repeat the exercise and then rest for ten seconds. This was done three times in all. The gym was something like forty yards long, so you can imagine how we felt after that exercise – 'knackered'. My first pre-season training there under Tommy Docherty was harder than any training I've done, before or since.

In the morning we did an eight-mile cross country run,

finishing with ten laps of the track, and in the afternoon we did the same again. After the drive of about forty-five miles home to Nottingham I could not get out of my car, and I will never forget Penny laughing her head off at me!

With Penny pregnant we started making plans for the new arrival. Only then did I realize the responsibility that marriage put upon a man, the bread winner. What would happen, for instance, if I was injured for a long period? There would be no playing bonuses then. What if I even had to finish pro football completely? From that period to the present day I have always been thinking of the future security of my family.

D-Day: Roger was born after a long and painful labour for Penny. Immediately afterwards she said, 'Never again', but in time, of course, that was forgotten. In my following game I scored a hat trick – my one and only – and it seemed as if I had done it especially for Penny and Roger. I was now a father as well as a husband, and like most new dads I was very proud of my son. I recall saying to Penny, immediately after the delivery, how clever I thought she had been. This amused her greatly, but to me she had been clever and still is.

3

Go North, Young Man

Sunderland, 1970-73

While I remained in Carlton-in-Lindrick along with Roger, to sell the bungalow and make the necessary arrangements for the move up to the north-east, David was a house-guest of Alan Brown. He was a little embarrassed and concerned at having to lodge with the manager for those first six weeks in Sunderland, as some of the players may have felt it was favouritism. New signings customarily had stayed in local hotels and boarding houses. However, it was very difficult for him to decline Alan Brown's invitation as the Sunderland manager was a very demonstrative and commanding figure whom people did not generally question or cross. For some unknown reason Alan Brown had an affection and affinity for David which encouraged him to welcome him into his home. Perhaps it was because of David's soundness and integrity and strong views on 'boozing' and infidelity which Alan Brown himself abhorred that enabled him to share his home so readily with Dave.

As kind as the Browns indeed were to David, he longed to be living amongst his own surroundings and have the household attuned to his likes and dislikes. Since David had been married he has shared my love of good food and has become something of a gourmet and an excellent chef. Mrs Brown, on her own admission, was not the world's best cook. Eager to please, on one occasion she enlisted

Dave's help by copying his personal recipe for spaghetti bolognese, which surpasses any other I have ever tasted. Unfortunately, when the meal was presented to the curious, impatient family, it was completely unrecognizable to Dave. Somehow she had managed, during the process of cooking, to alter the recipe to a rather revolting curry which no one was able to eat.

During those six weeks David did, not surprisingly, lose weight! However, I hope I do not sound malicious retelling that story, because Mrs Brown was a dear lady and it was kind of her to offer to have David staying. She even invited me to stay too, when we were first looking for properties to buy in Sunderland, and I found her a very warm, if slightly scatty, hostess.

We were fortunate in that we were able to buy a house in Sunderland into which we could move very quickly, legal transactions permitting. Undoubtedly Dave's experiences at the Browns' encouraged him to seek a hasty alternative that would not hurt his hosts' feelings. He could not very well ask to move to a hotel, as that would have appeared ungrateful, so the only solution was for us to find our own home as soon as possible. Perhaps, due to the quick, hasty decision we did not choose too well, but at that particular time there were not many available houses within our limited price range. Also the houses in Sunderland cost more than the same houses in Carlton-in-Lindrick; fluctuating house prices from area to area was a problem we were to encounter several times during our wanderings around the country. Sunderland did have a club house that we could have leased for a nominal rent, but having possessed our own home since marriage we wanted to keep the security of owning our own bricks and mortar as a hedge against inflation.

When we first moved to Sunderland in February 1971, the same month that Britain was launched into decimalization, we were very happy, despite the intense cold that greeted us. Even in summer on the north-east coast there seemed to be a perpetual cold easterly breeze coming off the North Sea, and I used to feel sorry for the holiday-makers on the beaches at Roker and Seaburn, sitting in their deck chairs, blue with cold but determined to enjoy themselves. It really is a shame that the weather is so unkind to that part of the coastline, as there are some beautiful picturesque beaches along it.

Having scored thirteen goals in League and Cup games for Rotherham during the first four months of that season as centre-forward, David was bought to continue to play in that position. He had hoped, initially, that Alan Brown had acquired him to play at centre-half, because that was the position he himself preferred. It transpired however, that Alan Brown bought him because he could play equally well in both positions, but since what they lacked at that particular time was height up front, Dave was chosen to strengthen the attack.

Unfortunately, after only three games for Sunderland, during which he was an instant success both with the crowd and with his fellow professionals, he was injured in the fourth and had to be substituted. That injury caused him to be out of the game for six weeks, and David was naturally impatient to return and prove to the Roker crowd that he was a worthwhile, long-term acquisition. This he successfully achieved, settling in quickly to become an ever-present member of the side.

He was still only twenty-four when he was transferred to Sunderland, and considering his belated entry into League football he had made remarkable progress. We were both pleased that at last he appeared to be one step nearer his goal, which was to play in the First Division. The thought of playing for England was still in the future, even though it had been mentioned in the Press by reporters, and by Tommy Docherty and Alan Brown. When Dave had signed, Alan Brown received a congratulatory letter on his 'good buy' from Tommy Docherty.

The house we bought was on an estate similar to the one on which we had lived in Carlton-in-Lindrick. We later made friends with a couple who lived opposite us and had a baby girl a few months older than Roger. The amazing thing was that one of them, Hazel, came from Stapleford, where David was brought up and where his family still live. At one time they were even in the same class at the local Albany primary school.

The local inhabitants were generally friendly, but it took me a long while to understand the way they talked. It was like living in a foreign country at times. Initially I used to stand in the centre of the shopping precinct in Sunderland just listening to the people talking as they walked by, often without understanding a single syllable. I could not comprehend the shop assistants and was forced to ask them to repeat, often several times, what they had said. Gradually I began to be able to translate the 'new language', and by the end of our stay in the north-east I had absorbed several local colloquialisms into my own vocabulary.

The players and wives at Sunderland would often socialize, independently of football gatherings, visiting each other in their homes and going out regularly in the same company. Most of the professionals' wives and girlfriends went to every match at Roker; it was a big social event for some of them. I was completely devastated and humiliated the very first time I went to watch David at Sunderland. It was a bitterly cold day and, unaccustomed to the piercingly cold breeze coming off the nearby sea, I decided to put comfort before fashion. I donned my duffle coat and jeans, and had my hair neatly tied in two pig-tails. I was growing it at that time and it had just reached the unmanageable 'in-between' stage. (Blow drys were not very common then, and back-combing was still the order of the day.) I did wear a little make-up, but not my full 'war paint'.

Before the game the players' wives would meet in the Roker Park Social Club, which was near the football club at that time. I think my horror was probably apparent when I was introduced to the other wives by Mrs Brown, as they were all, every last one, dressed up to the nines, complete with false eyelashes. They looked dressed more for a wedding rather than a football match. I had joined a glamour club, but no one had warned me. In a way I felt that I had let David down, though he assured me I had not, but I had wanted to create a good initial impression, and compared to them I felt scruffy.

After that, games would never be quite the same for me as there would always be the fashion parade beforehand, and being a newcomer I was anxious to conform. I know that I probably should have just gone to the games to watch the football and ignored it all, but I believe most women would react similarly in the same situation. I never have been vain, but I certainly do not like feeling shabby, so from then on I had to rack my brains each match day as to what to wear, and I bought a plentiful supply of false eyelashes.

Within the club there was a clique to which we, as newcomers, were not admitted. We were never really made to feel welcome by some of the players and wives, but David did forge a friendship with a player who was transferred to Sunderland just before Dave. Sunderland's tall Scottish full-back Dick Malone appeared at first glance to be fairly reserved and quiet, but in reality he was a rogue. Dave and Dick shared rooms when the club went away and the antics that the two got up to were often hilarious.

When the team returned from a pre-season tour which took them to Mallorca, Dave looked insipid and quite ill. This was not surprising after the following tale came to light. Both David and 'Tricky Dicky', as a contingent of the Roker crowd had nicknamed him, were not drinking men. The most alcoholic beverage Dave would normally partake of in those days was cider, but that was not readily available in foreign places. On the eve of the team's return to England they were all given the night off. Most of the players planned to visit some of the local bars and clubs and savour the night life in order to relax. Before leaving the hotel Dave and Dick had a drink at the hotel bar. When the waiter came to take their order they were undecided what to have. They had consumed rather a lot of coke while on the island, and by then were tiring of it as it tended to fill them with gas. Dick, remembering that he had once tasted apricot brandy which was fairly palatable, ordered two, one for David and one for himself. Both of them drank everything as if it was a soft drink, and the apricot brandy was no exception. After gulping the contents of their glasses they went to the neighbouring hotel. They entered it as sober as judges but within fifteen minutes were as drunk as lords, having swallowed four apricot brandies in quick succession.

It soon became evident that apricot brandy was too sweet to continue having all night, so the couple had to think of another drink. They discussed the possibilities and decided upon one bacardi and coke with an extra coke to drown the flavour of the bacardi, between the two of them. Well and truly inebriated, they started behaving boisterously, shouting 'Hey Jimmy!' at the Spanish waiters and ordering fresh drinks every time a waiter passed their table, which quickly became stacked high with new bacardis and cokes. From that hotel they managed to find their way to a night club where they sat in the corner and generally behaved badly.

Shortly some of the more accustomed drinkers amongst the players followed them into the night club and were amazed at the vision which greeted them. Never before had they witnessed Dave or Dick merry, let alone stone drunk and shouting obscenities. Suddenly Dave felt very nauseous, so he told Dick he was going to the toilet in the night club, but instead he made back for the hotel, leaving Dick behind in the care of Billy Hughes. At the hotel Dave went up to their room, which was on the eleventh floor, managing to stave off the nausea until he entered the privacy and sanctuary of the bedroom. He vomited copiously, but instead of doing this in the toilet as he would normally have done, in his drunken stupor he hung out of the window into the night air. The danger of this revolting act did not penetrate his befuddled brain.

Dick meanwhile, had decided to locate his friend, and also returned to their hotel. Just off the reception was the gentlemen's toilet, which Dick entered in search of David. No David, but while in there he decided to relieve himself of some of the liquor he had absorbed. To his horror the manager, Alan Brown, entered the toilet too, so Dick then had the task of appearing perfectly sober, as the retribution for being publicly drunk would have been very severe. He managed to urinate quite normally and made for his quick exit through the door. Panic! He pushed and pushed at the damn thing but it stood fast and would not budge. The sweat was by then pouring off him, and all he wanted to do was run, but he could not escape. As the manager approached Dick's heart throbbed in his chest, then Alan Brown proceeded to open the door quite easily by *pulling* it and walked past without saying a word.

The next morning, very much worse for wear, Dave and Dick ordered a coke. They had intended to try the old remedy of drinking a hair of the dog, as they felt so wretched, but all they could muster was to sit and gaze at the coke, which sat proudly in the middle of the table until Martin Harvey, their club captain, finally came to their rescue and drank it. On the aeroplane they managed to ward off the vomiting that their ever-present nausea threatened. At Newcastle they gingerly emerged off the aircraft and hastily returned home to their beds.

There were regular acts that Dick often repeated, such as winding the window of his car down in the midst of traffic and shouting stupid things at people, often complete strangers, across the road, or walking through the streets with Dave, the two of them jabbering away together loudly in an invented foreign language.

There was another occasion, again in Mallorca, when his imagination really ran wild. There was a party of Americans staying in the same hotel and on one occasion David and Dick found themselves sitting next to a couple of young ladies from the group, in the hotel lounge. Starting a conversation with them, Dick said he worked on the aircraft carrier which they could all see from the hotel in Palma harbour. He indicated that his assignment was 'top secret', but told them he worked on submarines, one of which was somehow incorporated within the aircraft carrier (some people, it would seem, are extremely gullible!). After elaborating the story, which his captive audience believed, for a further five minutes or so, he said, 'All right, I'll tell you the truth, we're really refuse collectors on an exchange with Mallorcan dustbin men.' There was no end to his fantasies. One of the girls said that by coincidence her father owned a large refuse collection business in America and that if they were ever stuck for a job to let her know.

The final tale I shall relate concerning Dick included Dave and his brother, Jack. When the team were in London one time, where Jack was living, the threesome went out shopping and parked the car in a multi-storey. It was the kind of car park where one is given a ticket on entry to produce when going out, so that the attendant can calculate the relevant charge. After completing their shopping they returned to Jack's car and made for the kiosk whereupon Jack frantically searched for his misplaced ticket. After a minute or two, still without any success of locating the ticket, Dick suddenly opened the car, acted very suspiciously and said, 'Okay, the game's up, let's make a run for it!' – pretending to have stolen the car. The attendant was speechless, Dave was giggling, and Jack, unaccustomed to Dick's antics, was for an instant worried. He hastily found the offending ticket and they all went on their way laughing their heads off.

To say that Dick was a real character is a gross understatement – there could never be another like Dick Malone. Dave was always forced to be a little apprehensive and on his guard when going anywhere with Dick, because he knew that almost anything was likely to happen, but the two of them were the best of friends throughout Dave's stay at Sunderland, and fond memories always spring to mind at the mention of his name. I always felt rather sad that his wife and I did not get on a little better, because the boys were so close that it would have been nice to have extended that warmth between the four of us.

There was a lot of back-biting amongst the wives at that time, and there were one or two wives who were 'social outcasts' and talked about in their absence. Initially I was allowed to encroach on the tightly knit pre-match gatherings of the wives, and we would occasionally entertain some of the players or visit them in their homes. For several months we saw quite a lot of Billy Hughes and his wife Linda. Linda was at that time not getting on too well with one of the other wives, and in an effort to mediate and bring them all back together we had several parties inviting both couples. But often we would be told, 'We're not coming if so and so is.' What could one do or say to that childish remark? However, we did eventually manage to bring them back together to share each other's company, but in time that would backfire on me personally and there would be a time later on when I needed Linda's support publicly but did not receive it. That hurt me a great deal – after I had stuck by her and helped her on several occasions.

Others also incurred the wrath of the 'gang of wives', and the feuding that occurred between some of the wives, all part and parcel of the Sunderland set-up, became quite obsessive and distasteful. I was happy to try and keep out of the thick of things, though eventually I was to be drawn into it and ultimately to become the main target.

Not long after our move to Sunderland we booked a holiday with my parents to go to Ibiza at the end of May 1971. All the preparations were made well in advance – I always like to be organized – but I had mixed feelings when five days before we were due to depart David was called up as a late inclusion on the England FA XI tour of Australia and Tasmania. They departed about the same time as our holiday began. Because of injuries to Malcolm MacDonald and Rodney Marsh, forcing them to drop out of the tour, the team was lacking in forward ability. Of course the representative opportunity could not be missed and hasty re-arrangements had to be made. I would still go on holiday with my parents, and Roger of course, and David's place would be taken by my friend from across the road, Hazel, who would take her daughter too.

David had to have all the usual vaccinations and inoculations necessary for a trip to the Far East, which were normally administered over a period of several weeks, but his schedule dictated that he had to have everything altogether. He was quite ill for a few days afterwards. Another problem was passports. I did have my own, but we had only had Roger's name included on David's. We had to dash to Liverpool to the Passport Office to have his name recorded on mine, but arrived at a few minutes before four o'clock – only to be informed that the particular person we needed to verify the alteration had already left the office, which was, even as early as that, on the point of closing. So, after driving all the way from Sunderland in a desperate rush, we still had to return empty-handed, without the passport. The girl in the Passport Office did say that the altered passport would be sent in the post the next day, but even in those days the mail was not particularly reliable. Dave had to leave to join the England FA party the next day, and if the passport did not arrive the following day it would have been too late for me to go on holiday. Fortunately the gods must have been with us because it did arrive in time, though I was not looking forward to going to Ibiza without Dave. It would have been our first holiday together since our honeymoon, as the previous summer we were unable to go away because I had been very pregnant with Roger.

Dave left to meet the rest of the party and I would not see him again for nearly six weeks. We were both worried about how Roger would react to the long separation at such a tender age. He was only eight months old, and we thought he might forget his daddy in that time – after all, six weeks is a long time to one so young. Fortunately for me, the time was broken up by the trip to Ibiza and I also went home to Nottingham for a while.

I wrote to David almost every day and he still has my letters. I missed him terribly, and this new experience was to give me a foretaste of the many international trips to come in the future. I was desperate to see him, and being so far away I was not even able to hear his voice regularly as the telephone costs were prohibitive. It is strange when one is parted for so long, one even begins to forget what the other person looks like. I did receive one phone call, however, and I was very excited when the phone rang on 21 June, our wedding anniversary, and I heard an Australian voice say, 'Adelaide calling, I have a call for you.' With so little time to speak one can never think of the right things to say, but nevertheless it was good to hear Dave's voice. However, I did still have quite a time to go before I would see him again, and I cried my eyes out when I had to put the phone back on the hook.

I believe the England FA XI was chosen by Sir Alf Ramsey, after nominations from clubs, and was considered to be a trial for many of the players whom he would normally not have been able to try out. The FA had a very productive and satisfying tour, winning all nine games, scoring thirty-four goals and conceding only two. It is interesting to note that Mick Mills, David's present England colleague, also played further forward on that tour and scored a few goals into the bargain. For Dave, personally, especially considering he was only a late inclusion, it was an outstanding tour, and he even managed to finish joint top scorer.

There were occasions in Australia when boredom, often a problem on such a long tour, engulfed the team, and one such bout resulted in David's room-mate, George McVitie, endeavouring to create his own amusement. The rooms had very large fans mounted in the middle of the ceilings, and George, lying on his bed, decided to throw someone's socks into the fan, and then clothes, and finally, after altering the speed of the machine to maximum, threw up pieces of fruit that were in the bedroom. The fruit was chopped into pieces and flung all over the room, and the resulting mess was considerable. Dave as usual insists that he was just an onlooker and never did know who had the job of clearing everything up.

At one hotel the guests were invited to hang out their breakfast orders on a printed card the night before. One morning when Dave's and George's breakfasts were brought in by the waiter, there was a full meal, with steaks, which Australian people often consume first thing in a morning. One of their team-mates had evidently altered their order the night before, when it was hanging on the bedroom door to be collected by the night porter.

For a professional footballer there is always the temptation to commit adultery – offered by unscrupulous girls, 'football groupies' as they might be called. I have never had to worry about my husband. I trust him completely and I know he has very strong views against married men committing these acts. When a couple of the married players at Sunderland confessed their stories of infidelity to Dave, he would just turn round and say, 'Don't you love your wife?' Do not misunderstand, he is not a prude, but he could never comprehend a happily married man wanting to jeopardize his marriage, nor could he understand the need to seek extra-marital relations. However, in Tasmania this behaviour must be considered normal, because, at the end of a function the England party had to attend after a match in Hobart, they noticed to their horror along the wall on the opposite side of the room a line of young ladies – hand-picked for them! Realizing the players had been away from their wives for several weeks, the hosts had obligingly provided these women to offer some relief to their frustrations. That was taking hospitality too far. Three or four of the players – Dave included, so he tells me – made a very hasty retreat, somewhat embarrassed by their hosts' innuendo.

It does not take much imagination to know how I felt when Roger, my parents and I travelled down to Heathrow to meet the very fatigued David off the plane from Australia. Of course Roger did instantly recognize his daddy, and we all travelled back to Nottingham, where we stayed for a couple of days before we three resumed our journey to Sunderland. It took Dave a couple of days to ward off the jet lag he suffered from the thirty-six hour flight. Even then we only had a short time together before Sunderland's pre-season training started, which included a tour to Denmark and more separation from the family. David never did manage to fit in a holiday that summer.

Life seemed to be ticking over quite nicely for us then, and the time appeared to be right to think about having a brother or sister for Roger. When he was twelve months old I conceived our next child. Though I wanted another baby, preferably a girl, the thought of another experience like that in Kilton hospital seemed daunting, so I decided that I would have this baby at home, where I could have Dave present at the birth. Hospitals still did not allow fathers to be present at delivery in those days.

We had planned to have the baby in May, at the end of the season so that Dave would be available. Of course, with my previous medical history some doctors might have preferred to have had me in hospital, but I was adamant that I wanted this baby to be brought into the world in the most loving and natural environment possible. Also, at that particular time Sunderland had a very capable, efficient flying squad to deal with any complications at home deliveries, so that a doctor, anaesthetist, blood, etc., could be at the patient's bedside quicker than in some hospitals.

Confident that the back-up team was at hand if necessary, I enlisted the help of the local midwives to ensure my home confinement. During my pregnancy I had developed blood-pressure trouble, and instead of making the regular trips to the ante-natal clinic I was able to have the midwives visit me at home for a time. One midwife, 'Sister Mac', who attended me in this period, became a firm friend and her son baby-sat for us.

The encouragement I received from David during my labour on that hot day in May was invaluable. I had studied the Erna Wright method of childbirth and with the help and comfort of the midwife, Mac, my delivery was one of the most pleasant things that has ever happened to me, and not many women who have given birth naturally could say that. I was able to cope extremely well using that method, and enjoyed every minute of it. Margaret Irwin, the wife of Cecil Irwin, who was still a Sunderland player then, came to help, but the doctor would not let her be present at the actual delivery, and I was a little sorry about that.

The whole household was in uproar when Heather was born. I had desperately wanted a girl to complete our family and I dread to think how I would have reacted if she had been a boy. I think it is quite likely that I might have rejected it. Seeing it was a girl, Dave bounded down the stairs in two strides and immediately telephoned Alan Brown, of all people – not my parents first, or his parents, but the manager! Dave was bubbling with joy at having witnessed the delivery of our daughter, and I don't think he made much sense except that I had had a girl. When he phoned my parents, who were in the middle of cooking their dinner – I had Heather at 6.30 p.m. – they just turned off the gas on the cooker and immediately travelled up to Sunderland to see their first grand-daughter.

Right from the start she was a wonderful baby; being 8 lb 8 oz at delivery she did not require the regular three- or four-hourly feeds but was quite contented to wait five hours or even more. Instead of the proverbial 'cup of tea', which is almost obligatory after giving birth, I celebrated with Cec Irwin by toasting the baby in champagne, while the rest of the 'team' cleared up.

A week or so after Heather entered the world, Sunderland were travelling to Italy to compete in an Anglo-Italian tournament, and in order to meet the team at seven in the morning to travel on the coach to Newcastle airport, Dave had to wake at around six o'clock. As Heather was still waking at between five-thirty and six for her early morning feed, we did not bother to put on the alarm clock the night before. I have never seen Dave in such a panic as he was that morning when my father – my parents were going to be staying with me while Dave was in Italy – entered our bedroom to tell us it was six forty-five! Heather had chosen that particular morning to cut out her early morning feed.

Dave moved like lightning, quickly dressed and hurried off, without breakfast or proper farewells, with my father who was to take him to the ground. They arrived at Roker Park just two minutes late, that is all. But Brown, a real stickler for rules and regulations, including punctuality, would not wait longer than he had said, even for his 'star' player. So Dave and my dad had to follow the coach to the airport, and even though the other players on the coach told Alan Brown that Dave was following, Brown would not stop the coach for Dave before its scheduled pick-up to collect a couple of other players who lived en route.

When it finally did stop Dave had to rush to the coach before it resumed its journey and slink on to it as quickly as possible. Alan Brown never said anything to David about it, but it just indicates how unbending a person he was. I can think of several players who would have just said 'Blow it' and not bothered to chase the coach as Dave did. For the sake of two minutes it was all a little unnecessary, and shows how some managers treat their players like schoolboys instead of grown men.

At that time the newspapers contained reports stating that David was the biggest Sunderland idol since Charlie Hurley, and quoting the fans chanting 'Watson is our king' and 'Watson for England'. It may be that this made some of the other players' wives jealous. Certainly the fans instantly took to David, recognizing a true fighter and dedicated player. He was never 'cocky' either, which is a common personality trait with strikers, less attractive than the quiet, unassuming manner of David. There is no doubt that Dave was thought of highly by everyone at Sunderland, not least the Roker crowd, and is even today held in high regard there.

Constantly talking about trivialities such as one's hair-style or the latest fashions did not appeal to me, and this meant there was little in common between me and the other wives. One wife in particular showed her resentment. Our lifestyle was 'superior' to hers in that we owned our own house, whereas she lived in a rented one at that time, and we were very happily married too. Those possibilities may not be the reasons that I was to be the recipient of her anger, and that of her cronies, but they are certainly the only answers I can offer, as I never gave anyone at Roker any cause to despise me as she so obviously did. I never flaunted Dave's success; as I have already said, I was his fiercest critic, and though I was proud of him I could still find fault in his game. Nor did I flaunt our better home; I have never waved that in anyone's face, and I have never been a snob. I have always enjoyed meeting people and have a friendly disposition enabling me to get on with most people. But for some reason I had transgressed and was to be ostracized from that time on.

It is very difficult to find suddenly that you have no friends when you are living in a strange place away from your family. The experiences I had to endure over the following two years were enough to undermine seriously my confidence, and curiously I became less articulate and more unsure of myself. There even came a time when I had to seek medical help for the depression that was forced upon me by that woman. The worst part was never knowing what I had done to warrant that painful exclusion. If I had known I could then have treated and hopefully resolved the situation. It all came at the worst possible time: just a few months after giving birth I was still very vulnerable and emotional, and where I should have received compassion, none was forthcoming. Jimmy Adamson, who later managed Sunderland for a time, was to make reference to the unsavoury element at the club. Those who had been at Sunderland knew what and who he meant.

Women can be bitches when they want to be, and I was to be on the receiving end of their viciousness too many times. I do not want to go into too much detail for fear of seeming petty and trivial, but an accumulation of continuous maltreatment and unfriendliness can seem unbearable, particularly without one's family being on hand to offer some support and reassurance. I tried my best to make things work, but when the other parties are unwilling to meet you half-way there is very little hope. I wrote to my main tormentor and even telephoned her in an effort to resolve the situation, which took a great deal of courage, but she would not talk to me.

Dave was unhappy, too, but to his credit he prevented his unhappiness from affecting his game. Inevitably, though, he asked in the end for a transfer to another club. It seemed the only answer, as we had done all we could to try to resolve the situation, but the club refused his request. Alan Brown did come to our house to talk to me and try to clear things up, but he was powerless too, though he did know about the vindictiveness in certain quarters. I wanted desperately to be accepted, heaven knows why, but after much heart-break and many tears I decided that it was just not worth the effort and that any future friendships in Sunderland would have to be outside of the footballing circle. But the problem was always there in the background niggling away at me.

Dave:

I had great expectations of Sunderland. It was the big time at last. I say 'at last', though in fact I had only been a professional for less than four years. From electrician to £100,000 footballer in that short space of time! Of course £100,000 was a tremendous amount of money for a player ten years ago. To me it was a fairy story come true.

Everything about Sunderland football club was big: the ground, the training grounds – seventeen acres all told, plus a gymnasium which was threequarters of the size of a football pitch – and, last but not least, Alan Brown, the manager. He treated me really well, and on many occasions went out of his way to protect me from the Press. I only wish that my four and a half years at Sunderland had been free of trouble.

4

We've Won the Cup!

Sunderland, 1973-75

The season of 1972–73 saw several changes at Roker Park, not least of which was the sudden departure of Alan Brown. He had always maintained that whoever took over from him as manager would reap the benefit of his careful planning within the club and achieve the success which had eluded him. He had, during his spell there, been responsible for the development of the club's wonderful training facilities at Washington, near Sunderland, and had also created a productive youth policy.

The gymnasium at Washington was extremely large, and in the future would be the venue for various indoor sports, including a televised display by touring Japanese gymnasts. When Dave first went to Sunderland the development was still to be completed and I can remember one pre-season when the players had to lug concrete about and help lay slabs for Alan Brown. That was supposed to be part of their training! Such was the character of the man that nobody dared refuse. I do not think many modern professionals would put up with that treatment.

Many of the players disliked Browny, for there was no doubt he was a very hard taskmaster and disciplinarian, but he was very straight and David never had any trouble with him. His departure gave the chance for the caretaker manager, Billy Elliot, to return David to his preferred position of centre-half. His first League game in this position was away at Carlisle, and I travelled in my own car, along with Keith Coleman's wife, to watch the game.

It was a bitterly cold day and the Carlisle ground is very open, so the freezing breeze made it very unpleasant for the spectators. Dave did not achieve what was expected of him in that game, but it had been a long time since his last game as centre-half and it was obvious that there was great potential waiting to be unleashed. Unfortunately the team did lose, but Billy Elliot stuck to his decision in the next game, and from then on Dave never looked back. The two years he had played centre-forward for Alan Brown were in some ways wasted years. I am not alone in my belief that had he been playing centre-half during that period he would probably have entered the international scene earlier. However, the seasons as striker were to give him an extra dimension, and his experience as centre-forward undoubtedly helped him when the opportunity came to go up front for set pieces and so on in years to come.

When Sunderland signed Bob Stokoe from Blackpool to take over permanently as manager, the whole team were pleased, for here was a man who was almost the opposite of Alan Brown. He treated the players like men and gave them freedom on the park which Brown had at times refused them. Brown used to say, for example, that only Dave could shoot within eighteen yards of the goal and players had to remain in their given territory for the whole of the game. Several players were to benefit greatly from the refreshing change, none more so than Billy Hughes. He and Alan Brown often disagreed about policies concerning play, and even on social occasions too. Bob Stokoe continued to play Dave in the centre-half position, and Dave went on to have one of his best seasons ever.

The beginning of 1973 saw the start of the FA Cup competition in which Sunderland were destined to play a major role. Dave played magnificently in the run-up to the Cup, scoring in several rounds. I went to see the team play in the semi-final against Arsenal, which was held at Sheffield Wednesday's ground. As many football supporters remember, Arsenal were beaten, the Sunderland team playing very well to earn a 2–1 scoreline. After the game the emotional scenes were tremendous; no Sunderland supporter wanted to leave the ground, but wished to stay and savour that win for as long as possible. Bob Stokoe was called out on to the pitch after the game and there were tears of joy from everyone. The rank outsiders and underdogs were through to the FA Cup Final, and even if they were not going to win, that in itself was a wonderful achievement.

The run-up to the final was very exciting. Suddenly the Sunderland team were big business and everyone wanted to know them. Firms were clamouring for their endorsements on products, and advertising offers were abundant. The wives, too, were involved in several promotional events, but I was never told of these by the wife whose job it should have been to inform me. Instead she would pass on a message via Linda Hughes. What should have been one of the highlights of David's career was severely marred, if not ruined, by our problem with the Sunderland clique.

The team went to stay at the Selston Park Hotel, which often plays host to Cup Finalists preparing for the big game. Arrangements were made for my two young children to stay in Nottingham for the weekend, but my parents were able to go to the match as they were to employ a babysitter. They had faithfully followed Dave's career up to then and were determined that they would not miss the opportunity of seeing their son-in-law walk out on to the famous Wembley turf. Of course no one knew then that David would in the future be fortunate enough to do that many times.

The wives travelled down to London the day before the

match, but as I had had to drop my children off at Nottingham I made my own way by train from there. Dave had received permission to collect me at the railway station and transport me to the Grosvenor Hotel, where we were to stay. By then my confidence was really shaken, due to the problem we had at Sunderland, and my nerves were stretched almost to the limit. I was quickly becoming a nervous wreck, which is not at all like me. Hitherto I had always been resilient and able to take control of situations, but the thought of me staying in the hotel that night with the other wives, the majority of whom seemed to hate me, began to get the better of me. Bob Stokoe knew the situation only too well – it was by then common knowledge – and Dave was very worried for me as he knew how I would feel ostracized and hurt if I was left in the hotel alone.

An unprecedented move was made that Friday night. In order to preserve his peace of mind, Dave stayed with me in our hotel room, with Bob Stokoe's approval, and slipped out of the hotel at eight in the morning so that no one would know, and returned to Selston Park. Such an arrangement would not normally be considered, and it serves to illustrate how bad things were for us. Probably because he was with me for the evening, Dave was able to put the Cup Final right at the back of his mind until the Saturday morning when he set about preparing himself mentally. He slept soundly, too, whereas, had he been at the team hotel, where the thought of the big game was dwelling on everyone's mind, he would more than likely have had a restless night.

I felt much better and comforted, though I was still dreading the trip in the wives' coach to Wembley. There was the inevitable fashion parade with many of the wives trying to outdo each other, but I had been a football supporter for many years, and to me the most important thing was the game of football. I did dress up too – after my first

Sunderland game I would never be caught in that trap again – but I could well have done without all of it.

I was very nervous and excited at the prospect of my husband walking out on to the Wembley pitch. I had often watched the Cup Final on the television at home, but nothing could have prepared me for the joyous atmosphere of that day. When our coach arrived the Roker Roar was in full song and they easily drowned the noise from the Leeds supporters. Almost every outsider, with only a few exceptions, presumed Leeds would win. However, the Sunderland contingent were, as strange as it may sound, completely confident that we would win. There was absolutely no doubt in our minds. But to many it was a foregone conclusion that the First Division team would triumph over the Second Division minnows.

The wives had a block of seats adjacent to the royal box, and Linda Hughes sat next to me. She, too, was a true football supporter and knew a great deal about the intricacies of the game, which is more than could be said for several of the wives. We were both very tearful when 'Abide With Me' was sung, the hymn of the FA Cup Finals, and could not contain our emotions as our men walked out in single file behind Bob Stokoe on to the famous Wembley turf. When our husbands recognized us in the massive crowd and waved at us, I was bursting with pride. They all seemed so relaxed and determined to enjoy their experience.

I can remember very little about the game, except that I was on tenterhooks the whole of the time and two minutes before the end of time, with Sunderland winning 1–0, Linda and I looked at each other and she said, 'I think they're going to do it, Penny.' We burst into tears of excitement and relief and these lasted for a good while after the final whistle.

When the Cup was held aloft the Sunderland crowd were [illegible]ic and we were not alone in our tears of elation;

many of the men around us were crying too. The Roker Roar had been very evident throughout, and I am pleased to say there were no ugly scenes of hooliganism before, during or after the game. The good spirits were universal. They have to rank as the best and most knowledgeable football supporters in the land.

After the traditional laps of honour the wives returned to their coach in Wembley coach park, where the champagne immediately began to flow. By the time we reached the hotel we were all a little tipsy, and even though the majority of the wives went straight to their rooms to dress for the evening banquet, I and just a few others including Toni Collins, the chairman's wife, waited in the hotel reception to greet our conquering heroes on their return. I was especially pleased, as David had performed magnificently and many reporters voted him the Man of the Match. We were jumping around our bedroom singing, 'We've won the Cup,' as happy as anyone ever can be, as we tried to dress for the evening's events.

The banquet, which was held in a neighbouring hotel, passed off successfully and without incident, and the players' wives were generously presented with mounted gold sovereigns from the club's directors for having had to endure the separations that the Cup run had caused. Everyone connected with the club celebrated that night, and to their credit, especially considering they had not been to Wembley since 1937, the club made sure that everything was catered for and appeared to know just how to look after us all, sparing no expense.

The following day, instead of the players and wives returning to Sunderland together, as would have normally been the case, the team had to go on to Cardiff where they were due to play an outstanding League game. That meant they would not return home until the Tuesday. After our good-byes, the wives went on to our coach and I was forced to sit at the back, as the 'gang of wives' had commandeered the best seats which had tables. The long journey back to the north-east was broken for the wives for lunch at a restaurant near Rugby. We all sat around one large, specially reserved table and had a fairly pleasant meal, but it ended in one of the worst moments with those wives.

The players were shortly to be taken abroad for a well-earned holiday, and it was put to the vote of the team to decide whether or not they took their wives with them. I am told that only Dave, Dick and a couple of others wanted this, while the vast majority preferred to 'have a good time without the encumbrance of their wives'.

During the meal the conversation turned to the proposed holiday, with several wives complaining that they never had the opportunity to accompany their husbands on such excursions. My ears immediately pricked up at this, and I saw a way of seeking a little revenge for the way they had treated me by pointing out that we had been given the option, explaining what had been said at the players' meeting. Of course I can see now that I was just being spiteful and it was totally wrong of me to elaborate on or even mention the conversation. Understandably I was shouted down by them; after all, no woman likes to think that her husband prefers to go on vacation without her. It would have been better for me to have kept quiet, but I wanted to try and hurt my tormenter. For once, however, I had not counted on the ferocity of her counter-attack. Most people who know me would probably find it difficult to imagine anyone 'getting the better' of me in a verbal contretemps, but I was already at a low ebb, my confidence shaken, and completely outnumbered, and she succeeded in humiliating me in front of everyone.

I did not travel all the way back to Sunderland, but was dropped off on the M1 near Derby, where my father had arranged to meet me as my children were still in Nottingham. On the Tuesday my parents took us all back home, and when we arrived at our house in Houghton-le-Spring, there was bunting tied up all over the street and house. The neighbours gave us a great welcome home, and there were congratulations from all sides. That afternoon the team were due back, and it had been organized for the wives to meet them near the A1 outside Sunderland, where we would all change on to the open-top double-decker which had been laid on for the victory procession to Roker. The streets were crowded with people of every shape, size and age. Little babies were hoisted shoulder-high by their over-zealous fathers and shaken almost like football rattles. The enthusiastic crowds lined the streets for miles, having waited for a long time, most of them dressed in red and white and holding banners aloft. The organizers had grossly under-estimated the turn-out, as the coach was hours late for its scheduled arrival at the football club, where the team were finally due to make a lap of honour. If supporters are the blood of a football club, then Sunderland should never require a transfusion.

The merriment lasted for days. There was a civic reception for the team in the new Civic Centre, and the team were invited to attend the function at which Bob Stokoe was given the 'Freedom of Sunderland'. The whole town was elated and businesses suddenly prospered and productivity greatly improved. However, the season did end on a sour note when Micky Horswill was sent off against Queens Park Rangers at Roker in the last outstanding League game, and the match had to be stopped for several minutes following a pitch invasion. For Dave and me, though, our private battle against the Sunderland clique continued and matters grew steadily worse.

Three and a half months after our productive visit to London another potentially serious blow was to add to our already mounting problems. It was necessary for me to be hospitalized for a biopsy operation on a lump in my left breast. For several days I had been bleeding from the nipple, but foolishly chose at first to ignore it, frightened at the implications and hoping it might go away of its own accord. However, after mentioning the problem to a couple of my friends I was bludgeoned into a visit to my GP. He immediately referred me to a specialist at the Royal Infirmary, Mr Jones, who made hasty arrangements for my admission for the operation. Although he insisted from the outset that he strongly believed the condition to be benign, nevertheless I was very worried – and understandably – about the possibility of my lump being malignant.

I was only twenty-three and the thought of a mastectomy at that age, or even worse, the thought – if I did have cancer – of leaving my young family without a mother, disturbed me greatly. My imagination really ran riot and although outwardly I tried to show I was confident, inwardly I was torn apart. After the operation I was much relieved to find I still had two breasts. This was hardly surprising, as I had never signed a consent form for a mastectomy and Mr Jones certainly would not have performed one without my signature. But one does not always think rationally at such times of stress. The biopsy did prove that the lump was benign: a fibro adenoma was the culprit.

This problem was to recur frequently in the future, but although there was no permanent solution no more operations were necessary. Some women are just 'lumpy' people, and I appear to be in that category. The lumps could have been removed but, as one doctor put it, 'We could keep hacking away for ever more.' I was prescribed medication to help the body get rid of any excess water, and I took these when the mastitis became fairly painful, but in the main they proved pretty ineffective so I eventually discontinued taking them. I do, however, have to keep a

Receiving the Novice Cup from adjudicator Constance Grant at Butlin's Holiday Camp, Filey. On the right is Miss Tozer, my dancing teacher.

Dave leaps high to score his first League goal against Crewe at Meadow Lane.

Tommy Docherty and his 1967–68 Rotherham team. Dave is second from the left in the back row, and our friend Dave Bentley is the player seated nearest to the right.

Sailing through the air for Sunderland with goalkeeper Jimmy Montgomery during the 1973 FA Cup Final.

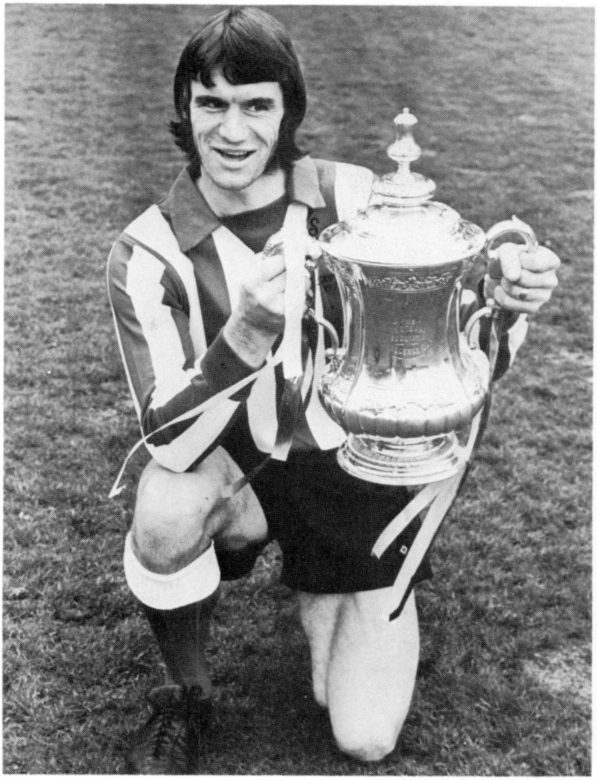

The Cup that cheers! Dave fails to keep a straight face as Dick Malone lurks behind the photographer.

Two Watson fans celebrate his selection for his first international appearance at Wembley against Argentina.

The wives of City on our way to Wembley. I'm third from the right, with Marie Bell on my right and the two Joans (Royle and Tueart) on my left.

Wembley 1976. My bloodstained hero hoists the League Cup aloft, with goalscorers Peter Barnes and Dennis Tueart.

England's No. 5! After Gemma's precipitate arrival Dave brought Roger and Heather to see us in hospital.

Bill Taylor sends Dave away early from an England training session on account of an ankle injury. In the background are Mick Mills, Trevor Francis, Phil Neal, Phil Thompson, Terry McDermott and Emlyn Hughes.

Dave with his new boss Lawrie McMenemy on the day he signed for the Saints.

Airborne for Southampton at Linfield during a recent tour of Ireland.

Two very different scenes on the Wembley turf. ABOVE: Dave and Steve Coppell kicking around with Rick Parfitt of Status Quo. RIGHT: A great moment for Dave as he leads out the England team for the World Cup qualifying match against Rumania in April 1981.

'Roger is going to get this dog wrapped round his hea if he doesn't let go of my toe.'

This book has a happy ending.

careful check – as all women should – and watch for any noticeable change.

The following New Year I was hospitalized again, with the same consultant taking care of me, but this time it was only for an uncomplicated appendicectomy.

After the euphoria of the Cup run, which had destroyed a few other clubs' reputations, I decided that, as Dave was at home such a lot and as I was becoming bored with domestic life, I would embark on a new career. Since studying the Erna Wright method of childbirth I had become very interested in midwifery, and my aim was to do that. However, in order to become a qualified midwife it was necessary for me to initially train as an SRN (State Registered Nurse). I applied successfully for entry into the February 1974 school at the Sunderland Royal Infirmary. I was chuffed to finish near the top of my class in the pre-training school (PTS), which was really quite an achievement considering I was one of the oldest there. Most of the girls had joined straight from school, and their brains were still accustomed to school work. I really enjoyed nursing, and even though it was demanding physically to run a household with young children and do a full-time nursing job, I think I coped fairly well. Dave has never liked hospitals, in fact he has always had a dread of them, but I used to rope him into visiting the patients, who got a tremendous boost from seeing him. He also donates blood, and has been doing so for several years.

Undoubtedly the FA Cup Final had been a stage for any prospective international player, none more so that David who had performed so well. He first heard that he was included in the England party when he was in Budapest where Sunderland were playing a European Cup Winners Cup tie against Vasas, and his first international game came in Lisbon, in April 1974 against Portugal which resulted in a 0–0 draw. He was included in the side because the regular centre-half, Roy McFarland, was out due to an achilles tendon injury, and even the Portugese Press raved about 'Watson'. It was the repeated injuries to Roy that would in the future give Dave the opportunity of playing for England again, but we were both a little disillusioned that Dave was so underrated and had to wait to be given the Number Five shirt only when Roy was out of the reckoning.

That was, however, the only game he played in an England shirt for Alf Ramsey. When Joe Mercer took over as the caretaker manager following Ramsey's dismissal, he was reluctant at first to play Dave when Roy was injured, as he had never seen Dave play. Against Scotland, in the home internationals at Hampden Park Roy was, once more, injured, so Joe Mercer was forced to name a replacement. Instead of giving Dave his chance to win a second cap, however, he chose Norman Hunter. After a disastrous first half England brought on Dave as substitute in the second half, and although they lost 2–0 Dave did enough to earn himself a place in the following international against Argentina at Wembley four days later.

I went to both the Scotland and Argentina games and I have never been to Hampden Park since. The atmosphere there is very threatening, and I honestly believe that most of the spectators do not see the game. From the evidence I saw of bottles of all kinds of spirits being passed from person to person – one was even given to me – and from the condition of the people swaying in their drunkenness, they certainly could not have seen the match clearly. It was a horrible, frightening experience, and I would be very reluctant to set foot inside that ground again.

The Argentina game at Wembley was very different. Once again I was bursting with pride when Dave marched out from the tunnel wearing his England shirt for the first time on English soil. He was very moved too, and even now when he lines up for the national anthem he experiences a tingling sensation right through him.

A successful Eastern European tour followed in which Dave played against East Germany, Bulgaria and Yugoslavia. Tommy Docherty's prophecy of all those years previous had finally come true. For almost four years before he was quoted as saying, 'Dave's the best I've seen in the air. He climbs higher than the best of them and he's accurate with his heading. On top of that there's nothing faster than Dave. He's got two very good feet, is a good trainer and a very nice lad. They talk about Roy McFarland and Larry Lloyd whenever the England centre-half position is mentioned but this lad could knock them all out of the way.' And a month before Dave was to be so instrumental in beating Don Revie's Leeds side at Wembley, Revie had said, 'I rate Watson one of the best all-round pivots in the country. He could give Roy McFarland a real battle for the England place.'

Alan Brown, too, had sung his international praises though perhaps he was more inclined to think Dave should fill the Number Nine shirt. Many people in fact had long since said that Dave should have been picked for the national side, but perhaps it was due to Dave's persistent failure to project his image that the first cap took so long in coming. Even now a lot of people would be surprised to know that Dave has played for England 63 times and holds a unique record of having worn the England shirt in thirty-three consecutive games, a record previously held by Bobby Moore with twenty-seven games. Indeed the margin would have been even greater had Ron Greenwood not been forced to try out Larry Lloyd as cover for Dave before the team went to Italy in the summer of 1980 for the European Championships.

A by-product of his inclusion in the England squads was that he was away from home even more. The normal routine before midweek games at Wembley or abroad is for the team to assemble on the Sunday and train together for a few days to get to know each other, so that means four or five days away from home, and of course a tour can be of several weeks' duration. Clearly that was an obstacle I had not envisaged when I had commenced my training for nursing. Initially my domestic plans went smoothly, but the more Dave was away the more I realized that I would have to sacrifice my training, as a full-time demanding job with such unsociable and erratic hours as nursing was impossible. In the end something would have suffered – either my home life or my nursing – so it was decided that, as the hospital did not want to lose me, I could continue on a part-time basis as an auxiliary. I chose to do two nights each week as I could put more hours in at one time that way.

I always seemed to get along well with the patients, and the fact that my husband was a footballer helped if we had a difficult youngster to cope with. As soon as I started talking about football they would soon come round, though often they would not entirely believe that my husband was Dave Watson and I would have to arrange for Dave to visit to prove it. I think, in the end he quite liked visiting my hospital, and if he had ever been close to becoming complacent about his success a visit around the wards to see the very ill would have quickly brought him back to earth. I realized too that life was very precious and all too short, and that the fact that one of the wives did not like me was pretty insignificant. Coming into contact with the local people I heard several stories concerning that same woman, and apparently she was not liked at all in Sunderland – even though she was a Sunderland lass herself.

* * *

Dave's main ambition had always been to play in the First Division, and although Sunderland were still in the Second he had managed on several occasions to represent his country. Following the Cup Final there had been repeated reports in the newspapers that other clubs were after him. Spurs were a particular favourite with the Press. However, his transfer request was once again turned down. Ambition coupled with our 'problem' had driven him to ask for a transfer. Sunderland failed to win promotion at the end of the 1973–74 season, and our great friend Dennis Tueart joined Manchester City. The Cup Final team was beginning to break up. After six months of me on night duty, Dave had had enough and he asked me to give it up. As Dave had decided to open a sports shop in Washington, I would soon be needed to help there, and with me sleeping a couple of days each week after night duty and Dave being away most weekends for football, we were seeing little of each other. The nursing, I reluctantly decided, had to go.

We had both resolved to stay and settle down in Sunderland and evidence of that was the sports shop. Sunderland FC had always been afraid that Dave would move on to another club if they failed to achieve promotion that season, and when David asked for a loan of a thousand pounds to add to his own money to help with the buying of new stock for the shop, they readily agreed. (He would be paying interest on the money, and it was all perfectly legal.) The unit was secured in the Galleries, a new shopping precinct, a manager found to run the shop in Dave's absence and the stocks were ordered. However, at the very last minute Sunderland pulled out, leaving Dave holding the baby. Fortunately he was able to withdraw from the lease of the shop and the sports companies were understanding, but David felt let down. Football clubs often talk about 'loyalty' which they dearly love to throw into footballers' faces, but loyalty has to be earned. Sunderland had behaved abominably and Dave was finally driven to ask for a transfer. This time he would not be put off by their refusal, he was determined to go. Finally the club did reluctantly capitulate, and he was put on the transfer list, though I do not think they ever intended to sell him.

However, a personal battle was now raging between Stokoe and Dave, and I knew who would win. Stokoe was quoted as saying that he would see Dave sweeping the streets before he'd let him leave Roker and that he'd jump off the end of the pier if any of his lads left. (Well, sadly, he did not carry out this threat!) It takes a great deal to rile Dave, but once he is incensed there is no holding him back. He was on the transfer list for several weeks, during which time we were living in limbo, not knowing what the future held for us. The Press even came round asking if there was any truth in the allegation that Dave and I were getting divorced. Apparently Stokoe had said to the newspapers, with the best of intentions, that Dave had asked for a transfer due to 'domestic problems' and the journalists had misconstrued the situation.

Finally, on a Friday in June 1975, over two years after winning that Wembley trophy, Dave and the children and I went down to Manchester where, after four and a half years with Sunderland, he signed for Manchester City. There had been whispers of several different clubs being interested, but when Manchester City were mentioned we secretly hoped that this move would materialize, as we already had friends and relations living there. Even though it was Friday the thirteenth, and on that same day our lucky black cat had been killed, they were not to be bad omens for us because we enjoyed living in Manchester – so much so, in fact, that we still think of it as 'home'.

The relief to be finally away from my 'prison' at Sunderland was tremendous, and I can never thank Peter Swales, the City chairman, and Tony Book, the manager, enough for giving me the opportunity to start afresh, let alone giving Dave the chance to kick his first ball in the best division in the world. Our marriage had had to endure a considerable strain during those troubled four and a half years, but we emerged at the end of it with a bond of love and understanding that was stronger than ever. Having survived that period we felt we would be able to survive anything that the future might hold.

Dave:

As Penny explains, there was a lot of trouble with the wives at Sunderland, and it was a fact that one of them never spoke to me for two years. What the reason was, I don't know. Being the type of person that I am, it did not worry me, but I knew that it upset Penny. When this girl finally did speak to me, something at the back of my mind flashed red, as if to warn me, 'Beware', and as it turned out my instincts proved to be right.

I remember one night Penny and I were dining with a couple of friends at a restaurant in Sunderland which we regularly frequented, when I noticed the girl and her husband together with another of the players and his wife. During the meal I looked in her direction and to my disbelief was greeted by a big fat tongue. She was actually putting her tongue out at me in public! I thought it was hilarious. Her husband did apologize to me the next time I saw him at training – but how childish!

The FA Cup run was fantastic but underneath the euphoria the problem was simmering steadily, and eventually, shortly after we won the Cup, it all boiled over. I think that changed my attitude towards a lot of people within the club, but even after all that happened we did stay for two more seasons, both times narrowly missing promotion into the First Division.

The season following the FA Cup win, Sunderland were of course into Europe for the Cup Winners Cup. In our first leg of the first round we were to play Vasas Budapest. I recall vividly browsing round the shops with my very good friend, Dick Malone, when Doug Wetherall and another reporter rushed up to me and told me that I had been included in my first England squad. I was genuinely surprised, and so delighted that for a moment I was quite speechless.

It was a different world meeting up with my first international squad. I was in awe of all those world-class players. I don't want to give the impression that my team-mates at Sunderland were not good players, but the England squad were the cream – and I was actually with them! It was not until February 1974 that I played my first game for England, and on that occasion I was so nervous that I was glad to finish the game, but after my England début I had no doubt that this was the life for me and that from now on my goal would be to command a regular England place.

5

Dropped by England

Manchester City, 1975–77

Our move to Manchester came at the best possible time, in the close season. David had completed his international duties, and before our family holiday we had a few days in which to visit Manchester in search of a new house. We had friends already living there who were able to chauffeur us around the outlying districts of the city – a great advantage when one is a stranger. As soon as we saw Hale, which is near Altrincham in Cheshire, south of Manchester, we decided that it was the place for us. The abundance of trees was comforting to us as we had missed them in the north-east, where it tends to be rather spartan; coming originally from Robin Hood territory, we were used to being surrounded with trees, and it really is true that one can miss them.

We saw something like thirty houses in three days; we were determined to go back to Sunderland with negotiations for a house under way. The first two days were unproductive, mainly because we were only looking at properties up to a certain price limit. The houses in Hale were much more expensive than the equivalent ones in the Sunderland area. We never seemed to move to a place where they were actually cheaper than our previous district!

On the third day after lifting our price limit, we saw several properties that were distinct possibilities, but we finally chose one in Carlton Road – mainly because it was in good decorative order and already empty, so we would be able to move into it as soon as the legal processes were completed.

We returned to Sunderland with a great weight lifted from our minds, to prepare for our well-earned holiday with the children in Tenerife. It had been on that luscious island, two years previously just after the FA Cup Final when Dave and I went on holiday without the children, that we first met our friends who live in Manchester. I cannot put into words how much our friendship with Tom and Hilda Whittaker means to us; suffice it to say they are the epitome of true friends, giving us support and love whenever it is needed. Our holiday with the children was a welcome break after the uncertainty of the previous weeks, and even though I realized that the removal to Manchester would involve me in a lot of work, the prospect seemed very attractive and I could hardly wait to return home and set things moving. We did encounter one mishap, however, while staying at the El Chapparel, which is a complex of apartments in the south of the island, with several swimming pools and a children's pool around which we spent most of our time. The pools were regularly drained and cleaned and were generally in good order. One day, however, Roger emerged from the kiddies' pool screaming his head off with blood pouring from a foot wound. Evidently someone, possibly the day before, had broken a pair of goggles in there and had said nothing to the attendant. Children had been playing in it all day without ill effect, but Roger had to be the unlucky one who found the broken glass.

For the first five years of his life he was never away from the casualty hospitals; he was so accident-prone that I used to be nearly demented with worry. The result of his latest accident was three stitches in his instep. The manager of the complex, Willy Braun, was very kind and considerate, and after that he did his best to see that we received the red-carpet treatment for the remainder of our holiday.

When we returned from holiday, David had to pack his bags and go to Manchester to meet his new team-mates and commence pre-season training. During the period before I moved down, he stayed in a small hotel not too far from the football ground, which the club regularly used for new signings. He was no stranger to a couple of the players: Dennis Tueart had been with him at Sunderland, and Colin Bell was in the England team with Dave. The children and I moved down at the beginning of August, Roger commenced school in the September, and things could not have been better.

The Manchester City club had a really friendly family atmosphere, which radiated right through from the groundstaff to the directors. It was quite different to the one which I had become accustomed to at Sunderland. The team were playing well and even though their away record left a lot to be desired, they were still a club to be feared by others visiting Maine Road. The pitch is kept in top-class condition at all times and it is one of the best in the country; the supporters, though perhaps not quite as vociferous as the Rokerites, made Dave, the club's record signing at £275,000, welcome to Manchester.

Only a handful of the wives went regularly to the games and the atmosphere in the tea room after the match was delightful. We had made it a policy, after the Sunderland affair, never to get too involved socially with players and their wives ever again. We had learned the hard way. I did see a fair amount of Colin Bell's wife, Marie, as she lived only a short distance away, but otherwise we saw the others at games, Christmas parties and official functions only. I was fortunate in that I was able to arrange a baby sitter immediately we moved to Hale, so I was able to go to the matches regularly. I had followed Dave and had seen him play more than any other person and I had no intention of missing him play in the First Division. He made his début in that division against Norwich City at Maine Road, where the home team won 3–0 and David was rated the star player in most of the Press reports.

The season progressed well, and life in Manchester was exceeding our wildest dreams. Dave's only worry was that Don Revie, the new England manager, might make drastic changes in the team, as 'new brooms' often do. But this fear turned out – at first – to be unfounded. At last everything seemed to be going well for us.

But one problem did arise: an injury to Dave which was to prove crippling and debilitating. Towards the end of his last season at Sunderland he had experienced a little back trouble; it was nothing of significance and he received a clean bill of health when he signed for City in the summer. However, his aching back grew steadily worse until it was unbearable, and the accompanying sciatica was excruciating. You might think from this that Dave complained to me, but he is not a moaner; in actual fact he is the complete opposite. He endeavours not to mention his injuries and says, after I have caught him out, 'I didn't want to bother or worry you.'

The injury reached a climax before the League Cup semi-finals against Middlesborough at the beginning of 1976. The nagging pain had never been far away, but in a training session prior to the first leg at Ayresome Park the complaint reached one of its intermittent acute phases. Dave has a very high pain threshold which enables him to carry on playing, sometimes foolishly, when most professionals would already have had to stand down. This time, however, even he could not stand the agony.

He was admitted to hospital, where he was given an epidural injection, into his spine, of hydrocortisone to alleviate the inflammation around the disc that was thought to be causing the problem. It was hoped that this would enable him to play in the second leg at Maine Road. However, the rather unpleasant injection, though it gave relief for a limited time, was not enough to withstand the rigours of a football match. We had bought an orthopaedic bed some months previously, and a period of bedrest was tried.

Occasionally the condition would subside a little, but it never completely went away. During the less acute periods – much against my wishes, as he was still in obvious discomfort – he would continue to play, but it was still troubling him so much that he could not even sit down at half-time in case he was unable to get up again. He had to lie on the floor to watch the television at home and the only comfortable way to eat a meal was to tilt his chair forward on two legs.

Clearly the condition would not right itself with the conservative treatment he had been receiving, but Dave was led to believe that continuing to play would not actually cause further damage (a view that would be disputed by a surgeon at a later date). So, the hero that he is, he played on.

A critical time was before the League Cup Final. The team had to endure a long coach journey to the training headquarters at a health farm on the Tuesday prior to the Saturday final. This aggravated Dave's condition, and that week he had to sleep on a board every night to get some rest from the pain. His training schedule had to be cancelled, and right up to the day before the big game there were strong fears that he would not be able to line up for the final. On the Friday, thankfully, the condition eased slightly and he was able to play, though he was still in considerable discomfort. It was decided that an unfit Dave Watson was better than no Watson at all, and he went on to play a significant role in City's 2–1 victory over Newcastle United to win the League Cup.

In the closing stages of the game, Dave received a gash, just near his eye, but as in many previous matches throughout his career he continued to play on with blood pouring everywhere. Even now his League Cup winner's tankard carries a blood stain inside from his dripping wound which he refuses to allow me to clean off. His rugged appearance is in the main due to the many facial injuries he has received playing football. It became so frequent at one time that Heather used to hide from him after a game, fearful of what she might encounter. The sutures were inserted by the club doctor, Dr Caprio, immediately after the game and televised by the covering television channel – another first for ITV!

Roger and Heather had both attended the game, though Heather was a little frightened by the noise of the Geordie supporters, no babysitter was available, and as my parents came to the game the children had to come too. This time the wives were separated and I was able to sit with my own family and friends, and even though the seats were not as good as those Sunderland had allocated their players' wives, it was nice to be able to share the triumph with my nearest and dearest. After the game the children went back to Nottingham, where they were once again staying with my parents. What would I do without my mum and dad?

The players and wives were staying, by coincidence, at the Grosvenor, though in almost three years between Sunderland's Cup Final and this one the hotel had altered a great deal and was not as good as I had remembered it. After the match there was a reception held in the hotel itself, but the main celebrations were planned to follow on the Monday after our return to Manchester. The reception after the game was, to be frank, not up to much, and I had expected better from a club like Manchester City.

The function on the Monday night was to make up for all that, and I thoroughly enjoyed myself. Each player was allowed to take two guests plus his wife, so in a way of a thank you to my parents we took them to share our rejoicings. The wives had been neglected somewhat and were not catered for as well as Sunderland's wives had been, and although I know one should not have made comparisons it was difficult not to when one had experienced comparable achievements at both clubs.

When we arrived at the hotel on the Friday it was stipulated that we were not allowed to have certain things, but our husbands instructed us to take no notice and to have anything we wanted and put it on the bill that the club would later settle. There was a little grumbling from certain quarters within the club, but nothing definite was said. Surely City could stretch to cooked breakfasts and room service? The day after the game we all returned to Manchester in two coaches, but the players went in a separate one to the wives instead of mixing with us as most people would have preferred. Previous City Cup Final winners had travelled back in a train, but we were relegated to a coach. The players were able to have some champagne on theirs, but for some reason the wives were forgotten, and we all arrived at the rest stop on the motorway rather peeved – especially at the sight of our husbands 'merrily' greeting us!

Arrangements had been made for the team and wives to watch the televised match, which was of special interest to me in view of Dave's stitches, but when we arrived there was nowhere to sit, little food left and we could not see the television. If that happened to the wives at Sunderland they would have been up in arms, but we all just accepted it as part and parcel of the general apathy at City towards the wives at that time. We all arrived after the long coach trip rather jaded to find it was expected of us to continue to the Town Hall and be officially welcomed back by the Lord Mayor, at that time a woman. The fans lined the route, but sadly nowhere near the number at Sunderland: Manchester is a divided city as far as football is concerned, and United have the upper-hand in quantity of support if not in quality!

The civic reception was a dreadful affair, with the Town Hall crammed with what seemed like hangers-on. The players had had a fairly late night celebrating, endured a long tiring coach trip home to be constantly pestered for their autographs. It was not the time or place for that. To top it all, the Lord Mayor did not even know the names of the manager and chairman of City, and in her speech got the two names reversed! We were all relieved to leave and and finally return to our own homes to rest after what had been a very strength-sapping weekend. Dave's back was bothering him, understandably, and as we were in for another fairly late night on the Monday evening we were glad to get into our own bed and catch up on some lost sleep.

During the evening of the Monday night celebrations, which were held in the Supporters Club adjacent to the ground, the wives were forced on to the stage, where we were publicly introduced and given bouquets (an idea Dave had instigated as a way of saying sorry to the wives).

With the celebrations over and League fixtures due to continue, the problem of David's back clearly had to be investigated further. The initial diagnosis had been a 'slipped disc' so the club sent him to see one of the country's top neuro-surgeons, Mr Richard Johnson, who conveniently practised at the Manchester Royal Infirmary. Mr Johnson arranged for David to be admitted to the hospital's private wing to undergo tests with a view to an operation to remove the trouble. He underwent an air myelogram. This means that a bubble of air is introduced into the spinal cord, rather like a lumbar puncture, and radiography then indicates any abnormality in the spinal column. The procedure is rather unpleasant, and even Dave had a moan or two. The nurse tried to comfort him by saying, 'It's all right Mr Watson, it's all right,' to which he replied, 'How the hell do you know what it's like?'

As is often the case following a myelogram, Dave was quite ill afterwards. The patient has to lie completely flat, with the foot of the bed tilted to make the head lower than the feet, so that the bubble in the spinal column will gradually disperse at the lower end of the spine. This takes a couple of days. If for any reason the head was raised, the bubble would rise to the brain and cause severe headaches. Even with careful nursing, Dave still experienced tremendous headaches and felt quite nauseous.

The myelogram confirmed that there was a piece of intervertebral disc protruding where it should not have been, and an operation was planned for the Saturday morning. The decision to have the laminectomy was entirely David's. He could have tried to carry on playing with all the discomfort and pain, but he would not have been able to play to his full potential, and there would inevitably be periods when games were missed. We were both apprehensive about the operation: after all, the spinal cord was going to be tampered with. As a nurse, and knowing all the possible though improbable complications that might occur, I was very worried. To make matters worse, while we were living in the north-east a Sunderland player, Martin Harvey, had had a similar operation which was unsuccessful, and poor Martin was forced to retire from the game. It appeared that the sword of Damocles was hovering above us. We were, though, very confident in Mr Johnson, and knew too that Martin had had an orthopaedic surgeon do his operation. There is much competition between 'orthopods' and neuro-surgeons regarding laminectomies, but I think the evidence is conclusive that, for the best possible results for a professional athlete, neuro-surgeons come out on top.

The day of the operation was one of the worst of my life. As I had been a nurse, one might think I would not be nervous, but in actual fact it works the opposite way. All I wanted was to be with Dave as quickly as possible after the operation and nurse him back to health. The operation took three and a half hours – longer than anticipated, for the problem proved to be much worse than even the myelogram had indicated. *Two* discs were involved, one of which had completely broken off and was protruding into the next disc's space. Mr Johnson was amazed that Dave had been able to walk about with such mobility, let alone actually play football, and he certainly would not have advocated continuing to play first-class soccer with a condition that could have crippled him. I was furious that Dave had been put into such a precarious position. I had never liked him playing when his back was so obviously causing him so much pain. Nature was saying that something was wrong and that football is not the most important thing in life. If anything terrible had happened I would have been the one left to cope – not the football club. Dave made a resolution then that in the future he would not put so much trust in what clubs said about any injury he might incur; from then on *he* would decide, regardless of pressure, whether or not he should play. That resolution, inevitably, was to cause him trouble in the future, but it must be stressed that he is not a shirker, and if it is at all possible for him to play a game, he will. I have known him start in games, or continue playing in games, when he has not been a hundred per cent fit following an injury, when other professionals would have sat on the side-lines.

This was Dave's first experience of staying in a hospital, and he coped very well, considering the gravity of his complaint. He did cause a stir a few hours after the operation when he was still very heavily sedated, when he was convinced he had not had the operation and kept insisting he wanted to lie on his back. He is a strong man and it took the nurses quite a time to calm him down – and not before he had pulled out his drip! When I arrived a short while afterwards, he had cotsides up on his bed. He *had* been a naughty boy! Another experience that I feel compelled to relate is rather embarrassing for Dave; nevertheless, I do have his permission to tell the story. After such an operation, the patient is bedridden for several days and has to gradually regain normal movement. The result of this immobility, as many patients will verify, is that the bowels become a little sluggish and constipation becomes a real problem. After nine days of bowel inactivity it was deemed necessary for Dave to have an enema. Dave, the big strong man I have told you about who can stand above average amounts of pain, could not stand the simple enema and demanded that the nurse extract the tube. He said that it was burning him. Perhaps the nurse had warmed the bag up too much, but nevertheless he did behave like a baby. He did not get his enema, though, and resolved the condition naturally. He was frightened to death when he did finally go after such a long time.

While in hospital he received many Get Well cards from supporters, friends and family; and the Manchester City players, along with Tony Book and the club's medical staff came to visit him regularly. He also received a very nice letter from the England doctor, Dr Burrows, who sadly has since died, and a visit from Les Cocker, Don Revie's Number Two, while the England Under-21 team were playing in the north. But a notable exclusion was Don Revie himself. He never even sent a card or a letter, which was his normal policy at that time. He had sent one to Colin Bell, and to several other England players, but not to Dave.

A slight element of doubt once again crept into my mind, and Dave's words about his initial reaction to Don Revie all that time previously suddenly came back to me. Though

Dave does not like to show any emotions, I know he was deeply hurt by Don Revie's lack of communication, and felt rejected. After all, he had won fifteen caps, and had even given blood for England and Don Revie: playing against Cyprus at Wembley he had received another facial injury requiring stitches but had insisted on carrying on playing. A visit from Don Revie, at a time when Dave had serious doubts concerning his recovery and his ability to play football again, would have been just the kind of moral boost needed.

The club sent Dave and the family away for a few days to Southport to convalesce, as Mr Johnson had recommended that Dave did nothing for three weeks, and he knew that if he was in Manchester, Freddie Griffiths, the club's very competent but sometimes over-zealous physio would want him to go down to the ground. Everyone at the club was very sympathetic and helped in every way possible. Tony Book has always been a kind, thoughtful man in that respect. Whenever Dave was away on England duty, Tony would ring me up to see if everything was okay at home, and he always sent a Good Luck telegram if Dave was selected to play. Small gestures like that can mean so much. The recovery period went very well and Dave worked hard to regain fitness. He had a new lease of life, now that his back injury was solved, and he was relatively free of pain. He had played for both City and England with disc trouble, albeit unknowingly, for almost eight months. Having never been completely fit, his best football was still to come. He was completely fit again in time for the 1976–77 season and looked forward to playing both League and representative football again.

Dave got his League football all right, but even though he was to play his best-ever season at First Division level, finishing as the Junior Blues' and Supporters Club's Player of the Year, the England honours did not continue. For reasons best known to Don Revie, Dave was snubbed time and time again, not even being included in the England squad, let alone the team. The Press, other managers, players and supporters all championed Dave's cause, but to no avail. Don Revie was unmoving. Even the Italian manager, Enzo Bearzot, said during that period, 'How is Watson? He is so positive and strong I would like a player like that.' The fact that domestically Dave was playing as well in what was a successful team – they went on to be runners-up in the League Championship to Liverpool with just one point separating the two teams – and even though there could be no doubt as to Dave's full recovery, Don Revie's England plans did not include David.

Publicly Dave commented that he tried not to let his exclusion bother him too much, but that was all a façade. Privately he told me that if Don Revie ever did ask him to play again for England he would tell him what he could do with his cap. That was not just said in a fit of anger either, because when Don Revie finally asked Dave to play again after fourteen months in the international wilderness, Dave's initial reaction was to refuse.

Tony Book rang up to inform Dave that he had been included in the England team and Dave said, 'Thank you very much, but no.' Tony tried to reason with him, but for several hours the answer was still the same. Finally, however, he did come round, and I was instrumental in persuading him to alter his decision. After I had reasoned with him for a couple of hours he changed his mind, but he did it more for me than for anything or anyone else. He had last played – against Portugal – in November 1975, and was recalled in February 1977, almost a year after his operation. Whatever the reason was for Don Revie's exclusion of Dave, he must have changed his mind, because even though England lost that game against Holland, Dave was to be included in his future plans after all.

* * *

The Watson family was to hit the headlines again in November 1977, but not for anything concerning football. In 1972, after the birth of Heather, David had had a vasectomy operation, because we felt at that particular time that two children was all we could financially afford. At that time, of course, the FA Cup success and England honours were still in the future. We had both continued to adore babies, and it was not for the lack of parental desire and affection that we made the big step to halt our family at two children. However, neither of us regretted Dave having had the operation as the freedom that followed it – the knowledge that I was not going to conceive a baby – was most enjoyable. Neither did Dave feel any less a man. Gradually, though, success had given us the material things we had never been able to envisage, and it became clear that financially we would be able to provide well for another addition to our family.

While Dave was in hospital having his back operation he took the opportunity to consult a surgeon who specialized in, amongst other things, vasectomies. Mr Garland, though prepared to try to reverse the vasectomy, warned us that the chances of success were slim. But thanks to his skills the reverse vasectomy did prove to be successful and we could plan to increase our family at some future date.

When it comes to birth control, the best laid plans can go astray, and we were taken a little by surprise when, in April 1977, I found that I was pregnant. Of course we were absolutely thrilled, but we would have preferred to have waited another couple of years, as I had resumed work and had managed to secure a fabulous job which I greatly enjoyed. I was secretary to the chairman of a public company which conveniently had its head office in Hale, and I had looked forward to two or three years in that employ. Nevertheless, the powers that be had mapped out in my personal plan that I should have a baby in 1977, and I was so grateful to be given the opportunity to experience pregnancy again.

I did have a few minor problems during my expectancy, but it was my third child and most of these were to be expected. The main inconvenience was that I suffered a prolapsed womb, a condition which proved to require rectification by surgery at a later date. The pride I always felt when I was pregnant and carrying Dave's child, and the excitement of the prospect of a new baby after we had never dreamed it was possible, outweighed any problems.

The child was due to make its entrance into this world towards the end of November 1977 – right smack in the middle of the football season! Once again I wanted Dave to be present at the delivery, though he had not been so insistent himself this time to witness the birth. I found out why later. As nature had been tampered with – first when he had his vasectomy and then when it was subsequently reversed, he was very worried that the baby might be abnormal. However, I did persuade him that I needed him at that time, and he had to concede.

On 16 November 1977 England were playing a World Cup qualifying game at Wembley against Italy, so we waited with bated breath in case the baby decided to appear early. Needless to say I did not go to that game, which was one of the few Wembley matches I have missed. The consultant obstetrician, Mr Richard Martin, a lovely fatherly figure of a man whom I was consulting privately, was persuaded to induce the baby on Sunday, 20 November, to ensure that Dave could be present.

The induction was something I would not relish having to go through again, but after an epidural anaesthetic the delivery was relatively painless. Considering it was my third child, it did last quite a long time – nine and a half hours, in fact – but my deliveries have always dragged on a bit.

The country's Press, who had been informed of the impending delivery and details of the case history, were impatiently phoning the hospital on that Sunday. Mr Martin was marvellous with them, even when one turned up at the delivery suite pestering him and wanting to interview me immediately after the birth. When Gemma was born, a perfect little girl and the image of her sister, we were all delighted. A miracle had happened, and we were part of it. The following day the flood of newspaper reporters and Press photographers arrived armed with bouquets – probably as a form of bribery to gain access! Dave had quite a job keeping them at bay and under control. The hospital staff were wonderful and helped a great deal. In the end the reporters were allowed in all together so that only one tiring session would be needed.

Partly because of the age gap between her and the other two children, and partly because she was wanted so much, Gemma did inevitably get spoiled and proved in the future to be quite a handful. She has never been a good sleeper, and during the first two years of her life I could count on one hand the number of unbroken nights we had. She has always been very active and forward for her age, wanting to be doing things – and sleeping just seemed to interfere with this! Maybe *she* could do without the rest, but the other members of the family certainly could not.

She was walking around the furniture at six months and actually walking unaided at eight and a half months old. How wonderful, some might think, but I can assure you that a delay in her mobility would have been appreciated. There have been times when I have wished, momentarily, that the reversal had not been successful, but of course those moments have been brief and soon dispelled when our little auburn-haired girl, our little gem, has done or said one of those wonderful heart-rending things that only a child can. It was difficult at times, though, to ensure that

Dave received a good night's rest, without being woken up, before a home game. If he was woken, however, it certainly did not affect his performance.

The summer of 1977 had seen Britain celebrating the Queen's Silver Jubilee, but during the many street parties and festivities the England football team were playing far afield in South America. Being four or five months pregnant, I was subdued that Dave was away for three weeks at that particular time. The inevitable boredom crept into the squad during the tour, and this time David and Dennis Tueart would be the culprits of some mischief.

Brian Greenhoff, Stevie Coppell, Dennis and Dave were in Dave's room one afternoon playing cards. Large creamy cakes were ordered but by the time they arrived the appetites had diminished. Dave was persuaded by Dennis to smell his cake - only to get his face pushed into it. His retaliation was to throw one at Dennis, then everyone started flinging cake, with cream and crumbs ending up in the curtains, on the carpet, in each other's hair and everywhere possible. It never ceases to amaze me how men, when put together in a group, resort to what can only be described as childish antics. However, it was good fun while it lasted and they did endeavour to clear the room up, washing the walls, curtains and carpet using the hotel towels. It took well over an hour to get the room back into some sort of presentable state - and three days, despite repeated shampoos, to remove every trace of grease from David's hair. Thankfully their cake fight had not been interrupted by anyone, so the hotel never knew.

After the England summer tour of South America, the footballing world was stunned by the sudden exit of Don Revie. The thought of a new manager brought a little fear and trepidation that Dave might once again find himself in the international wilderness, as a new manager might have a different opinion as to who should wear the Number Five shirt. However, as history has shown, Ron Greenwood was set to give Dave more England caps than he had previously received from any other manager. At least he was able to settle down, though not to become complacent, in the knowledge he was England's Number One centre-half and would be so for some time to come.

During the 1977–78 season Dave was given the honour of captaining Manchester City – something we both treasured – and as City did go on to qualify for Europe his captaincy did not prove unsuccessful. Off the field he worked hard as captain to achieve several concessions for the players and their families. Up to then, the wives were unable to get a half-time cup of tea, something which could have been much appreciated in cold weather, and after a game had to go out of the ground through the normal exits amongst all the pushing and jostling crowds, even though there was a convenient exit through one of the press boxes straight into the football club. David was able to arrange that this exit would be used by the players' wives if they wished to obtain half-time refreshments and a comfortable exit after the matches.

He also arranged Christmas parties for the players' children, with help from the other lads, at which Father Christmas would appear. The first year a suitable fellow was not available, so as he had no children of his own at that time, Dennis Tueart dressed up, but a wise Danny Donachie saw through the disguise, and at subsequent parties a more suitable Santa was found. Dave became known as 'Mr Fix-it', and if the lads ever wanted to buy anything they always asked Dave first, if he could put them in touch with suitable people who would 'look after them'!

As the captain's wife I tried to make new players' wives welcome at the club, and made a point of introducing them to the other wives. When Kaziu Deyna and his wife came to the club Dave and I did our best to help them settle. I thought the club did not do enough for the Deynas at first, and it was Dave who pestered the club into arranging English lessons for Kaziu. We visited them on several occasions to see if there was anything we could do to help them, and entertained them at our home in an endeavour to make them feel welcome. As they could not speak English and we could not speak Polish it was sometimes quite a strain, but I think we did help them to establish themselves in England.

Dave:

What can I say about Manchester City that everyone does not already know? It was one of the biggest clubs in the country, with a lot of star players – some of whom I knew – and the stadium was magnificent. After only three months of my first season at City, Colin Bell, the idol of Maine Road, was tragically injured in a League Cup match against Manchester United at the City ground. That injury was eventually to finish what had been a great career of a great footballer. England found it very difficult to replace him and, significantly in my opinion, failed to do so in time for the qualifying rounds of the World Cup.

Nevertheless we did go on to win the League Cup, beating Newcastle United 2–1 in the final. Not long after that game I was admitted to hospital for disc trouble. I had been having pain for around six months and it had slowly worsened. In fact I had had a ten-day lay off just after Christmas and missed both semi-final games against Middlesbrough, but that only relieved it temporarily. The week of the Cup Final I did not train until the Friday morning because of the pain in my back and legs.

However, in the final itself it gave me no trouble and I had a good game.

In hospital it was decided that I needed to have a disc removed, and thankfully, the operation was a great success. To this day I have not had any further trouble with my back. I realized then that I had had a narrow escape: the surgeon, Mr Richard Johnston told me that if I had continued playing football I could have ended up a cripple, as nerve tissue, once damaged too badly, can no longer repair itself.

Nothing I could say about Manchester City would be complete without a mention of Peter Swales, the chairman. For me he was and is the best chairman in football. If I had any problems of any kind he always tried to help, and in my business dealings he helped me by giving me some good advice. I know that at most football clubs the players rarely have much to do with their chairman, but at City, for me at least, it was wonderful having someone like Mr Swales to turn to for advice.

6

Plain Sailing

Manchester City, 1977–79

The season of 1977–78 seemed pretty uneventful, though City did of course qualify to play in Europe. Life at home was running smoothly, and by then David had started a couple of business ventures in the Manchester area. One was an agency which we formed with our close friends, the Whittakers, and his other interest was in furniture leasing with another dear friend, Eric Barnes, Gemma's godfather, who already had several retail shops in the north-west, trading under the name of Woodland Furnishings. Now in his early thirties, Dave had already started to think seriously about his life after football and made several plans to help ease any worries in that direction. He started a very complicated but hopefully fruitful pension arrangement that would give some sort of income immediately after retirement, but the businesses were also necessary if we were to maintain the standard of living which we were now enjoying.

The taxman was taking something in the region of eighty-three per cent of David's wages, and though some people might say, 'Well you must be earning a lot for that amount to be deducted,' there comes a time when one actually seems to be penalized for one's achievements by the heavy tax deductions. Where is the incentive in that? Footballers are in a unique position, too, because even though they do, on the whole, receive fairly good wages, they are taxed through the PAYE system, whereas other professions in the entertainment world tend to be treated as self-employment. This means that there is very little, if anything, that the footballer can claim back off his tax. There are no such things as company cars, mileage allowances or any of the other fringe benefits that so many people enjoy. Even when a player changes clubs his new one is not allowed to pay, or even contribute to, estate agents' or solicitors' fees. The only thing that the Football League permit is for the new club to pay the removal fees. Many of the fringe benefits mentioned that are part and parcel of the normal business world are prohibited, not by the government or the clubs, but by the powerful administrative body of the Football League. Often a footballer has two legislative bodies to contend with when working out his contract: the taxman and the Football League. It can be very frustrating when a club actually wants to give a player something, and is quite entitled to, according to the law of the land, yet is prevented from doing so by the League.

The end of the 1977–78 season saw David asking for a transfer from City. It was not that we were unhappy in the north-west, nor that Dave wasn't enjoying his football. The reason was purely financial. Dave had made his mind up that in order to ensure and protect our financial future he would have to play either in Europe or the United States, as the financial rewards in both those places were incomparably better than in England. The tax systems were infinitely more attractive, too, so a player could keep much more of his earnings. The Manchester City chairman understood Dave's feelings but was reluctant to see him go. I think I am right in saying that David was one of his favourite players, and it is true that they shared a special relationship. Mr Swales had always been considerate to me too. The foreign clubs were reluctant to pay the high fee that City demanded for a defender, so a move was not forthcoming.

Dave could have sat it out and waited, but in the end he was offered a new and very lucrative contract from Manchester City and we put all thoughts of moving out of our minds. We had never really wanted to move: the children were settled in good schools; Dave had commenced his businesses; we had simply been forced to think that way by his crippling tax bills. We were at least feeling settled, for the rest of our lives, and intended to stay in Manchester permanently. But as everyone now knows, something was to happen in the not-too-distant future which, much to our sorrow, would alter all that.

The following season saw Dave suffer another serious injury, one which even threatened to finish his career. For a long time, curiously enough, it was to be a well-kept secret from everyone outside the club, but eventually the problem was made public – though its seriousness was never indicated. For some unaccountable reason David developed some kind of a muscle strain, the origins of which were never traced. It forced him to limit his training, as he could no longer do sit-ups, up to that time he was accustomed to doing two hundred at each training session. It affected his kicking, and it even affected his love-making. City were very concerned, as indeed we were, as the condition remained and showed no sign of improvement.

At one time the club flew him to London to see a sports injuries specialist, but even he could offer no definite diagnosis. He was given a hydro-cortisone injection, but this only gave limited relief as it was difficult in such a condition to pinpoint the trouble. One diagnosis offered was that the ligaments that bound together the two sets of stomach muscles had been torn. However, the problem continued to the end of that season and troubled Dave continuously, even when he was playing for England. He had fought hard for the Number Five shirt, though, and would not give it up without a fight. The injury only caused him to miss a handful of games, as he continued to play through his pain. By the end of 1978–79, however, he was convinced that he would not be able to go through another season of top-level football with that injury, and was sure his playing days were approaching a premature end. Gradually, though, it began to clear up on its own, without any further treatment, and to disappear as mysteriously as it had developed. Even now, though, he does still feel a tenderness in that region in cold weather, and he still has to take his sit-ups easily – he only does fifty at a time now!

Living in the north-west was as pleasurable as ever, and the whole family looked forward to a long stay in the region. We had not counted on Malcolm Allison! It has to be said that right from the word go the majority of the playing staff were apprehensive at his appointment. The club were going through a lean time, it is true, but they had been playing well even though the results were going against them. Besides, clubs often go through rough patches, and the majority see their way through it eventually. The general feeling within the club was still good, and the players' morale was fine. However, in an attempt to stop the slide, Peter Swales brought back Malcolm Allison to revitalize the club. What a joke that turned out to be!

Obviously Mr Swales had the best of intentions: there has never been any doubt that first and foremost his main concern is for the club, and of course Allison had been successful during his previous time there. But that was a different Malcolm Allison. After a while, many of the players and staff who knew him from the first time commented how he seemed to have changed. Dave was wary of him right from the start. Much has been written about

Malcolm Allison during his second spell at City; better qualified people than I have tried to analyse his motives, so I do not think there is any point in saying too much now. He was similar to Tommy Docherty in that his best results had been achieved with a young team around him, though his record could hardly be compared with the Doc's. Allison's track record speaks for itself.

Right through the club the atmosphere changed to one of suspicion, and the place swiftly became miserable. Allison's arrival had promised so much, yet very little was achieved. His training methods, by all accounts, were boring: run, run, run, all the time, often around Wythenshawe Park, so that the players did not see nearly enough of a football. This excessive running aggravated Dave's stomach trouble considerably, and could well have been a contributing factor to his prolonged injury. He became so bored with Allison's training that the England sessions assumed new and monumental importance to him. At last the variety was offered again – ironically by the same coach City had forced out of a job, Bill Taylor.

My estimation of Tony Book greatly diminished during that period. He seemed to lose all influence at the club and to put up with very poor treatment. The players became very unsettled and the transfers are all history now. Brian Kidd, Peter Barnes, Asa Hartford, Mike Channon, Gary Owen and Dave Watson. It reads like a *Who's Who* of soccer. Yet during his time at Maine Road there were frequent comments in the Press about the deflated prices at which he sold these players, and the inflated prices he paid for their often unknown and unproven replacements. What he must have done to the balance sheet at City, once one of the most financially stable clubs in Britain, just does not bear thinking about. The Press and the football experts continued to try to analyse his reasoning without much success, but who really knew what was in his mind?

Not long after he was appointed as City's 'chief coach' England had a mid-week game at Wembley, to which Allison went. It had been arranged for him to bring Joe Corrigan and Dave home to Manchester after the match, as Tony Book wanted the players back in Manchester that night instead of letting them return the following morning, after a good night's rest, as some managers prefer. It was at the time that Allison was trying to make his first signing, Barry Silkman. Apparently after the game he was attending a function in the Wembley Conference Centre when someone told him that the Silkman deal was off because the lad had failed a medical. At that Allison just took off, leaving no message for Joe or Dave. He was, I believe, also supposed to have been attending another function, but missed that too. By the time Dave and Joe had found out that they had been abandoned it was too late for planes or trains to take them to Manchester. Their host at the Supersports function arranged for them to have his chauffeur-driven car after he and his wife had returned home, so the poor driver had to make an unexpected trip to Manchester. Being the hosts, however, they could not leave the function until all the guests had gone, which was around midnight, so Dave and Joe did not arrive home until just after four. Tony Book had wanted Dave to go into the club that morning, but I refused to wake him. The poor lad had played a hard game the night before and spent most of that night dashing around looking for transport, and had then had to face a long drive home. I was furious. It makes much better sense – and must be far safer when such distances are involved – to stay the night and travel refreshed the next morning.

Most of the players that Allison transferred were glad to get away from the club, but I could not help feeling very sorry when he transferred Gary Owen, who did not want to move. I have heard that Gary actually cried when he was forced to leave City, and I can well believe it.

By the summer of 1979 Dave had made up his mind that Allison and he did not belong together. The saddest decision Dave has ever had to make in football was deciding to leave City. His decision to move the previous summer and the subsequent change of mind had, we thought, at last given us some stability in life. We had sincerely believed we would stay at City until Dave's playing days were over. All of us wanted to, but Malcolm Allison made it impossible for Dave to stay. Excepting the times when Dave was injured, or excluded from the England team, I had never seen him so miserable. Almost every day when he came home from training he would grumble and say he could not put up with Allison any longer.

It was not that Allison worked the players too hard: Dave has never shied away from that, and his dedicated attitude has always earned him praise. Even Bob Stokoe said, on Dave's transfer to City, 'I believe Manchester City have bought a top-class professional who is a tremendous athlete and an extremely dedicated player.' In 1975 Mr Swales described him as 'a dedicated professional who is an example to all young players. He is also a great trainer and a wonderful player to have at City.' More recently Kevin Keegan said in his book, 'Watson is a late developer ... but he is so fit and determined that he should have no problems in staying at the top until he is thirty-five or even a little older. In training matches, we say, "Get Dave Watson on our side, and they can have the next two picks." We reckon him worth two men, because even in a five-a-side friendly on the eve of an international he'll want to win every ball.'

I hated Malcolm Allison for what I could see he was doing to Dave and to Manchester City. Dave and I talked it over and the only solution was to put in for a transfer in the hope that a foreign club would be interested this time. The thought of transferring to another English club was inconceivable to us, as that would have seemed in some way disloyal to City, the club which had been so good to us over the four years we were there. A couple of clubs in the Football League did make approaches for Dave, but he had made up his mind that Europe was his next goal. It seemed premature to contemplate playing in the States; he was still very much involved with playing for England, and his place would have been in serious jeopardy had he gone to play in North America.

However, we did not know then that perhaps we might have been advised to listen to the old proverb, 'Better the devil you know, than the one you don't.' The devil we had to encounter in Germany made Malcolm Allison seem like a choirboy. It turned out to be a case of out of the frying-pan into the fire.

His transfer request resulted in City selling him to the West German Bundesliga club, SV Werder Bremen. The high increase in pay was a bonus for us, but the main objective had always been to escape from Allison. Initially I had wanted Dave to try and work it out with Malcolm Allison, but my attitude altered when I could see that gradually he was destroying Dave and Dave's love of the game. A player must enjoy what he is doing to achieve maximum performance on the field of play. Amongst European countries, German soccer is, perhaps, the most in tune with that of Britain. Anxious to keep his England place, Dave readily agreed to sign for Werder Bremen, where the financial rewards seemed unbelievable. The stage was set for the next phase in Dave's career.

Dave:

With the arrival of Malcolm Allison there was a great feeling among the lads who had known him from his previous time there that our luck would change. Alas, it did not, and in my opinion the club was never the same. It was the end at City for all the players who had made a name for themselves – all the internationals. The first to go was my big mate, Brian Kidd. It had not taken Kiddo long to see what was going on. After him, it was a steady stream of the top players.

When I left to go to Germany it was a sad day for Penny and me as well as for the children. For Penny, because she was leaving a lot of friends; for the children, because they were being uprooted from school; and for me, because I had thought that I would stay in Manchester for a long time. I think those four years when I was playing for City were the happiest years of our lives.

No other club in this country could replace City for me, and I felt that America was not the place for me at that particular time, for the reasons Penny mentions. It was to the continent, therefore, that I was looking to go.

7

Stormy Passage

SV Werder Bremen, 1979

During April and May of 1979 I was quite ill with some mysterious intestinal disease, which had taken six weeks to diagnose and treat effectively. In that time I had lost a considerable amount of weight and was in desperate need of a recuperative holiday, so a 'holiday of a lifetime' was booked for us all in the United States of America, after David's international duties were over. Unfortunately, the holiday did not measure up to our expectations and we were beset by every mishap that could possibly happen – from our luggage being lost to a taxi we were travelling in catching fire! Gemma was miserable throughout the trip, from a combination of the travelling and the humidity, and the only place we were all really happy was Disneyworld, which was fantastic, in the true sense of the word. In Florida we found ourselves staying at the same hotel as Terry McDermott and his lovely girlfriend, Val. Their company was much appreciated on what had fast become a disaster of a holiday for us.

One good thing that did happen while we were away was that our house in Hale, which had only been put up for sale one week earlier, was sold – so that was one obstacle to moving to Germany out of the way. We arrived back in Manchester in the morning of 10 July, exhausted after the long flight home, and collapsed into our beds. My parents had arranged to come up to Hale on the following day to look after the children for a few days while Dave and I went to Bremen – he to report for training and me to look for accommodation. When we had first visited Bremen for Dave to decide whether to sign for them, he had stipulated in his contract that the club provide, rent free, a suitable house. This, they had assured us, would be ready for us on our return from holiday, so that we could move over to Germany as soon as we liked. Not only was the house not ready, but they had not even started looking for a place!

There is no doubt that the Germans had gone overboard in their efforts to obtain David's signature on our first visit to Bremen during the middle of June. Their hospitality was overwhelming, and the coverage the deal received from their national newspapers was indicated by the huge press conference called immediately following the conclusion of the discussions.

We were greeted at the airport by the manager of the club, Rudi Assauer, his wife Inge, the club's president, Dr Baumer, and Mr Pastor who was the head of the agency arranging the transfer, together with a huge contingent of pressmen. That evening we were wined and dined in a special private dining-room in one of Bremen's hotels at which Rudi, Inge, Dr Baumer and the agents attended. We were both made a great fuss of and generally made to feel like real celebrities, and it became clear from what was said that the club were banking on David becoming a huge attraction approaching the scale of Kevin Keegan, who played for their rivals and neighbours, Hamburg.

After our holiday, when Dave and I returned to Bremen, I had to take the matter of finding a house into my own hands. When asked why no accommodation had been found, their answer, as we were to find so many times in the future, would be 'kein Problem' ('no problem'). But it *was* a problem – certainly for me, if not for them. I had planned to stay in Bremen only a couple of days, as I had thought our new house would be ready for me to inspect, and that we could choose carpets, and so on, while I was there.

The manager's wife, Inge, a typically tall, sturdy German Hausfrau, took me under her wing, as she had promised to do during the first dinner in that private dining-room. She had told the president and all who were present that she would be delighted to help me in every way possible, and she would help me buy things for the house and generally settle down. She spoke quite good English, and as I could not speak German this was obviously going to help. The club only had two or three unsuitable properties for us to look at, which had been hastily found, I suspect, in the local Press. When I suggested to them that it might be a good idea to consult an estate agent, one would have thought I had put forward something quite remarkable. It had never occurred to them to enlist a professional's assistance.

Now my plight was becoming desperate. I had to return to England, because my father had to resume work, and it would be some time before I could go back to Germany. As I have mentioned, the club were obliged to provide a house, they did not want to have to purchase one, as their club capital would then be tied up in property, so they proposed to rent one. However, it became evident that there were no suitable rented places available, and I was then tempted to look at properties to buy. We were in luck, for although a lot of haggling had to go on between the vendor and ourselves, we found a house that was ideal for our needs, in a pretty German village called Kirchlinteln, close to the children's new school.

So, somehow, we were manoeuvred into buying our own house. The club did make some cash adjustment to Dave, but nevertheless owning our own home did prove to be quite a stumbling-block when we finally decided to return to England. The house was very sturdy, having been newly built, with the best possible materials, by the vendor for his daughter who was getting married. She, however, had then decided she did not want to live so near her parents, and he had been forced to sell it. It had a very large basement area, with several rooms, and we decided to have an extra bedroom and en-suite bathroom put down there for ourselves. It was a split-level house, which from the front looked like a bungalow but from the rear like a house. It was not as big as we had had in England, nor was there as much land, but we had expected to have to make a few adjustments living in a foreign country. The house prices were much higher, but we reasoned with ourselves that we would be living there for a couple of years, and that the investment in property should prove worthwhile.

I said a sad farewell to David and returned home to England to make the removal arrangements. Even though I was going to be seeing him in three weeks, he was far away over the sea in a different country and somehow that made the separation much worse for us. I left a very sorrowful and despondent-looking Dave at the airport, and I wondered then if he was beginning to have second thoughts. I must admit I shed a tear or two on take-off and on landing at Heathrow, though for some reason I was all right during the actual flight. After that the task in hand soon took my mind off our enforced separation.

When moving house within England there are a hundred and one things to arrange, and I had gained plenty of experience of it during our ten years of marriage. When moving to another country, however, especially, if you are planning to take everything with you, there are a *thousand* and one things. Dave, was of course, well out of everything and could offer little assistance, so I was left with absolutely everything to do. I was left to cope with legal documents for exporting goods, arrangements for export packaging and removal, change of address forms, forms from the Bank of England, hasty visits to vets for injections and yet more forms for the dog's exportation. Forms from the Electricity Board, arrangements for cars, alterations of insurances, visits to dentists, opticians and doctors. . . . I also had to fit in normal end-of-term school activities such as Speech Day, several family birthdays, a wedding and birthday parties that the children had been invited to.

All this and much more, had to be dealt with in three and a half weeks as we had planned, after assurances that the alterations on the new house would be completed by then, to move on 9 August. Dave, as usual, was hating hotel life, and I felt it my duty to try to be with him as soon as possible. The furniture removers needed two full days to export-pack all our belongings, so they started work on Monday the 6th. There was also the normal running of the household with three children; the washing did not wash and iron itself, and my offspring also had to be fed.

To make matters worse, fate decided that right in the middle of all this turmoil, my father, on whom I depended a great deal as he was an accountant and company secretary, should have a serious car crash involving a lorry. One good thing to emerge from his untimely accident was that Dave flew home for a fleeting visit to see Pop in hospital, so we did see each other earlier than expected.

There were, too, the many goodbyes I had to make, none more poignant than the one to our doctor, Joe Jacovelli. Joe is something of a well-known character in Hale. We always found him the best GP we had ever had and probably ever will have. He was such a good diagnostician and was so considerate in a brusque sort of way. He always popped in to check that things were okay at home when Dave was away playing football – completely off his own bat. How he managed to fit so much into his timetable never ceased to amaze me.

Somehow, everything was completed in time, and we were packed up and ready for our great new adventure.

My next-door neighbour had very kindly taken care of our sleeping and eating arrangements for the last two days, as our house was without the necessary. We had said a remarkably cheerful farewell to my parents, whom we had always been used to seeing so regularly but from whom we would now be separated for much longer spells. Dave, after having to use much persuasion, had managed to obtain permission to return home to accompany me and the children to Bremen. The club were not too happy about this, they expected me to manage with all our luggage, the three children and a connecting flight all on my own.

While I had been frantically making all the arrangements, Dave was installed in a local hotel in Bremen and was beginning to adjust to his new way of life. However, even he did not envisage that he was expected to change so much. People tend to imagine that German football is super-professional and that everything is catered for, right down to the last detail. While that might be the case at the majority of Bundesliga clubs, it soon became apparent that Werder Bremen were lacking in several major areas, areas that are probably taken for granted in English football.

The facilities 'back stage' were very poor. Generally the football clubs do not own the stadium in which they play, these are usually the properties of the local authority who cater for several sports at the same venue. This is why the magnificent stadiums with running tracks around them are seen so frequently in Germany. The rooms that the football club can use are allocated by the authority, and it is up to the individual club to negotiate what rooms they require. Apart from a couple of offices, dressing-rooms, one tiny laundry room and small masseur room, little else was provided. To Dave's astonishment there was no treatment room and there was not even a club physiotherapist! All English clubs – even Fourth Division ones – have treatment rooms equipped with all kinds of aids. This omission did not seem all that significant to him initially, but it was to prove an important factor when he became injured in only his second game for the club. An indication of the lack of facilities is perhaps best illustrated when I tell you that the players had to take home their own socks and towels to wash after training. Can you imagine, England's current centre-half rubbing away madly trying to clean his socks in his hotel bathroom!

The majority of his new club-mates seemed to accept him from the start, and several could speak English, which was a great help. Rudi, the manager, had also introduced him to an English tennis professional who lived in Bremen, called Mike Cole. Mike and his English girlfriend, Sally, took Dave under their wing the first couple of weeks, until I moved over, and during our stay in Bremen we became good friends. They had lived there for three years so they both had a good command of the German language and helped us a great deal with translations from time to time.

Before I had actually joined him, Dave admitted to me his reservations about Werder Bremen. Clearly they were not the club he had thought and the petty rules and regulations were depressing him. He wanted there and then to return to the English League, and although, as it turned out, it would have saved me a lot of work if he had done so before our mass exodus from England, I persuaded him to give it a fair try in Bremen. Trust me! I should have kept quiet!

9 August arrived, and we made our way to Manchester airport, where we would catch a flight to Heathrow for our connection to Bremen. Tom and Hilda, our old and trusted friends, were with us at the airport, and when our flight was called and it was time to say farewell we were all overcome with emotion. Though we tried not to, Hilda and I could not hold back the tears and even Heather, who absolutely adored Hilda, cried. After we had made our

way through airport security we bumped into the Manchester City team who were returning from a game abroad. It was a welcome opportunity to say good-bye to the many football friends we had made during our stay in Manchester. Tony Book, who was walking along with Malcolm Allison, shook hands with us and wished us good luck, but Malcolm Allison said nothing. When we walked to the plane we could still see Tom and Hilda waving us good-bye, and as the plane taxied to the runway tears once again welled up into my eyes. I wondered then when we would next see our friends, whom we had seen so much of over the years and who had been so good to us. I hoped with all my heart that this was one friendship that would not fade with the passing of time. All the happy memories of our life in Manchester came flooding back to me, and the first real pang of regret overcame me.

We arrived in Bremen, rather travel-weary, to find that our luggage, once again, had not been put on the plane and was somewhere at Heathrow Airport. What a welcome! A little to the local Press's and my surprise, there was no welcoming committee from the club this time. Obviously that had been a ploy reserved for our initial visit to Bremen to create a favourable impression. In fact Rudi and Inge were away on holiday. I didn't see her for over a month, and felt rather let down, as she had said she would be available to offer assistance. Was this the way of things to come? I wondered.

Despite continuous assurances to the contrary, our house was not ready on time. (The Germans do not need to talk about British workmen. It was eleven days of persistent geeing along before our home was habitable.) Reluctantly we moved into the hotel where Dave had been staying. Naturally the children found it inhibiting having to stay within the confines of our hotel, especially as the weather was warm. They could not understand the television, and boisterous games were not permissible as there was the other guests' peace and quiet to consider. The hotel manager pointed out a recreational area nearby belonging to a golf club, but he said that he was sure it would be all right for my children to use it. To relieve the boredom, when Dave was training and we were virtual prisoners in the hotel without transport or knowledge of the area, I would take the children for walks to this park for them to get some fresh air and exercise.

We had hoped that the house would be ready for when our own furniture arrived from England, so that this could be laid out in the appropriate rooms as it arrived. Dave had previously chosen the carpets that would be ready to be fitted immediately the workmen moved out. The day the removers were due to arrive we were at the house waiting for them, but as the hours ticked by it became obvious that something had happened. We made a phone call to the agents in Manchester who regretfully informed us that they had not heard anything from their men. As night started to fall we decided to travel back to Bremen. Our new home was some distance away near a place called Verden. On the Autobahn on the opposite side of the road we eventually saw our furniture van, which had broken down!

We really seemed to be going through a spell of bad luck at this period. The following day, mobile again, the van brought our belongings to our new house. However, the workmen were still engulfed in the alterations and the furniture could not even be unwrapped because there was so much dirt around. All that the removers could do was to pile the furniture into a couple of fairly clean rooms and keep everything in its packing. The club, who had ensured the completion of the house on time, apologized and offered Dave future assistance to put the furniture out and remove all the packing when the workmen finally did leave us. However, when that time did arrive poor Dave had to lug the things around for himself, for in spite of the offers of help from the club, none materialized.

One other question which arose through the house not being ready was what to do with our faithful pet, Tina? She arrived four days after us and a hotel is not the place for an alsatian used to freedom. I doubt that dogs were allowed anyway. Mike Cole came to the rescue; thankfully Sally was mad about dogs and they took care of Tina, who became quite attached to them until we were able to have her.

The day after we had arrived in Bremen, Dave went away for a game at Munich against Munich 1860. Even if it had been a home game he would still have been absent for the night, as the Germans take their teams away the night before every game, home or away. Some clubs in Britain do this too, but the majority prefer the players to have a good night's sleep in their own familiar bed. On the Saturday, which was a glorious day, Mike and Sally came to take the children and me out for the afternoon into the huge Berger Park in Bremen. We had a lovely time feeding the ducks, and the children and Tina enjoyed the freedom of the open space.

Unfortunately we were soon stunned by the news Mike heard over the German radio. Bremen had lost 4–1, but worse still, Watson had been sent off! I could not believe it when Mike translated the commentary that Dave had been given his marching orders for fighting. It was so out of character. It was a very gloomy Dave who returned to the hotel that night. The one consolation was that the club were going to back him all the way and that in their opinion, and the general opinion of the Press, Dave did not deserve to be shown a red card in the incident with the Munich player, Bitz. Several German newspapers actually expressed surprise that nobody had had the foresight to warn Dave about Bitz's reputation for getting opponents sent off! We ourselves received several letters from football fans asking why his team-mates or trainer had not told him of Bitz's reputation.

When I saw the replay on the television I was astonished that such an action was punished at all. Certainly in English League the result would not have been a sending-off. A strong talking-to or at the very most a booking, but that is all. Bitz, a small player (aren't most of the trouble-makers in soccer?) had lunged towards Dave as if to butt him. To prevent this happening Dave pushed Bitz away with the flat of both his hands. Then the amateur dramatics began and Bitz fell to the ground.

Some of the worst tackles Dave and I have ever seen are allowed to go unpunished in Germany, but nobody had warned Dave that the one thing the Germans will not permit is contact with the hands. The outcome of the red card was an eight-week suspension and a fine of 5,000 DM (£1,200). The club manager and Dave made a personal appeal at the hearing for leniency and to state his case, but each offence and subsequent penalty is listed in a book of rules and regulations (the Germans love them), and their 'football bible' stated that an offence involving contact with hands is punished by a suspension of eight weeks. Though they were very sorry, and were aware of Dave's special case, they could not bend the rules.

Under normal circumstances I do not think Dave would have even pushed Bitz, but his dissatisfaction with many things at the club and his pent-up emotions culminated in that action. The whole attitude towards players was completely different to England. Some players in Britain think that they are treated like children by their clubs, but they should spend some time in Germany: then I don't think they would be so quick to criticize. At Bremen they are almost encouraged to be jealous of each other. If a player missed training for some reason, the whole team was lined up and told why that player was not there, and the absentee list was meticulously checked until all the absentees were accounted for. In England, I am told, if someone does not turn up for training nobody takes much notice. That is a matter between the manager and the individual player concerned. At Bremen things were extremely regimented, and nobody dared question anything. If the players were told to report at a local shop to sign autographs in what was supposed to be their free time, they were expected to do so.

That was another bone of contention – free time. When Dave had first visited Bremen he was told training hours were similar to England. The reality saw them training at nine o'clock in the morning until lunch-time and then for two or three hours in the afternoon, but they did not commence their afternoon sessions until three or four o'clock. That was not so bad for the players who lived locally, but we had chosen to live forty kilometres away, so that we were near the military school in Verden. Most of the players went home for lunch and an afternoon nap, but Dave had to bide his time in Bremen. A couple of times he did come home for an hour or so, but the travelling he had to do proved too tiring. Leaving the house at 8.30 am, and sometimes not returning until around seven o'clock, meant he saw too little of the children, who mean so much to David. The day after a game, normally a rest day in England unless a player is injured, was another training day for Bremen, and many friendly games against local non-league teams were all part and parcel of the German football scene. The Germans pay well, but by God they expect blood for their money! Of course Dave never expected it to be a holiday, and he will work as hard as the next man. Nevertheless he could not help feeling he had been induced to sign for Bremen without knowing all the true facts.

Those friendly games against over-enthusiastic teams often resulted in injuries, and it was one such injury which eventually was the final straw for Dave. In only his second game for Bremen, which was another pre-season friendly, he sustained a fairly minor knee injury, but because of the apparent lack of medical knowledge the condition was allowed to escalate. Dave did play a couple of games with the injury, but the fluid developed around the joint gradually increased. He went to see the club doctor, who had his surgery between Verden and Bremen at another pretty village called Achim. It was well equipped, with its own mini-operating theatre and all kinds of medical gadgetry; but he and Dave did not see eye to eye over the treatment of football injuries. It was Dave himself who had to suggest to him that the knee needed some ultra-sonic treatment. One would think that after a club has spent so much money to purchase a top-class player and to pay him a high salary, they would want to carefully look after their investment.

Some German clubs do have physiotherapists, but unfortunately David had chosen one without this very important member of the back-room staff. He had simply taken it for granted that Bremen would have one. After his sessions at the doctors, he was still expected to travel all the distance to the football club, just so that the other players could see him make an appearance. Of course that problem does not arise in England, as the treatment is generally given at the grounds. It all seemed so infantile and petty to someone like Dave.

Another example of this pettiness arose when one of the players was married. A stag night had been arranged unbeknown to Dave: the player must have said in German in the dressing-room that he wanted everyone to attend his stag night on such and such a date and his English-speaking team-mates had forgotten to translate this message for Dave. The day of the stag party arrived, but knowing nothing about it Dave just dressed after training as usual and said good-bye to make his way home. 'Where are you going?' 'Home,' Dave replied. 'But you must come to the party; everybody must come to the party.' The trainer, Wolfgang Weber, was most insistent. Dave explained that he knew nothing about it, and could not join them as he was expected home.

Dave was then made to go up to the Presidium (the equivalent of our board) who were having a meeting in the football club. They all pleaded with him to go to the party, saying that if the public saw the Werder Bremen team all out together without Dave Watson it would look as though he had been excluded on purpose, and that there was possibly bad feelings amongst the players towards him. They then sent for the player whose party it was and gave him a reprimand for not having invited Dave, but Dave really was not bothered anyway. The poor player! It was all a misunderstanding and really very trivial. Dave did not go, though, for in any case at that particular time we had someone staying with us from England.

We were both astounded at the lack of privacy their players endure. Home addresses are published in football magazines and consequently fan mail arrives at the player's house, as do fans themselves on occasions. One's phone number is brandished around and the Press were always pestering us at home. Believe it or not, one reporter even telephoned in the early hours of the morning! Probably in the hope of catching Dave off guard so he might say something controversial.

The small village we lived in which was surrounded by agricultural land and woods, was a very pretty and friendly place. We all took to our life in Kirchlinteln right from the start. Only a couple of days after we had finally been able to move into our house, three soldiers from the local British army camp in Verden came to introduce themselves to us and to offer us practical assistance. It had been arranged that Roger and Heather would attend the English school on the camp, but the beginning of term was still two weeks off. One of the soldiers, Sergeant Major Bobby Duncan who was the camp's PT instructor, suggested that the two older children might like to take part in the summer play scheme which was being run by the Toc H. During those two weeks they were taken to several interesting places, and were also able to become acquainted with their new school friends. Tina, our dog, was loving the life in the countryside, especially her romps in the woods, and generally things at home were going well.

The language did not create any great problems, though it did cause a few amusing and exasperating moments. For weeks I tried to buy some disinfectant, but when I took the item home I soon found that I had made a mistake. This went on for several weeks until, finally, I enlisted the help of one of the army wives who kindly brought me some English disinfectant from the NAAFI.

As I have mentioned, at the crucial time during our first few weeks in Germany, Inge, the manager's wife, was not available to offer help with the language when we were choosing curtains. The company the club had put us in contact with to buy carpets and curtains had no one who could speak English but by then David had picked up a little kitchen German. Unfortunately he had acquired the habit of saying 'ja' to almost everything which he thought he understood, but when the curtains arrived we soon found, much to our dismay, that he did not comprehend as much as he had thought – for almost every curtain was wrong in some way or other. It took several weeks to sort everything out before finally, with the aid of a German dictionary, we managed to communicate properly.

The club offered little assistance, but thank goodness for

the enormous aid the army gave to us. They arranged for me a babysitter, a charming girl who was the daughter of a sergeant, and a cleaning lady, one of the soldier's wives and with the children settling in at school a normal routine was soon achieved. We were all gradually learning the language, I through shopping, the children through playing with neighbours' children, and Dave through his colleagues.

Dave returned to England during his suspension to play against Denmark at Wembley, a game England won 1–0, and although he had not played football for a few weeks he gave a good account of himself. Many of our friends and relations had taken that opportunity to see Dave again, so after the match they all had an impromptu party in the hotel near Wembley. Thank goodness for that game of football! Dave was becoming more disgruntled with his problems at Bremen, and the suspension made matters so much worse. Initially the club were very sympathetic about his sending-off, and they paid the fine for Dave, but the fact that he could not play for another few weeks made his trip to England even more significant. More than once during his career his England sessions would prove an escape valve for his footballing problems.

As the end of the suspension approached, Dave was anxious to play for his club again because it had become abundantly clear during the past weeks that he had joined a pretty bad footballing side and they desperately needed Dave's experience to help them start winning games. However, three days before he was due to make his comeback, disaster struck. The suspect knee was aggravated in a training session and blew up like a balloon. There was no way that even he could have played, but the club's reaction was anything but sympathetic. In Germany the manager or trainer decides whether a player is fit to play, not the footballer himself, and they decided they would take David with them to the away game against Schalke 04. In England an injured player does not generally travel with the team to away trips; he is usually left behind to receive further treatment.

However, the treatment, such as it was, that Dave was being given did not seem to be working at all. English clubs offer their injured footballers all-day intensive therapy in an effort to regain fitness as quickly as possible, but at Bremen Dave was receiving only an hour's treatment each day. Dave was becoming more and more frustrated and disillusioned as he lost confidence in their methods of treatment. The club were adamant that he should travel and Dave knew that if he did go they would probably make him play in the game. So he refused point blank to travel with them and that proved to be the beginning of the end for Dave at Werder Bremen. By now he did not care at all what the club might threaten to do, as he had had it with them. He sincerely believed that if he did stay with Bremen that he would be finished as a footballer by the end of that season, mainly because of their attitude to injuries and their poor medical facilities. If they could not cope with a simple 'footballer's knee' injury, he felt, what sort of problems would a serious injury cause?

When he was summoned to the club before a full Presidium meeting he was prepared to be reprimanded, but not as severely as he was. For failing to travel with the team he was fined 5,000 DM (£1,200), and even though initially they had backed him regarding the suspension and paid his fine for him, they then decided to discipline him for that and make him pay that fine too, a further 5,000 DM.

Worse still, the following week England were due to meet Northern Ireland, and even though it was in his contract that he must be released for England games, they told him he would not be able to go. They decided to recoup the money for the carpets and curtains, which contractually they were obliged to provide and had paid for along with other items in the house. Dave returned home completely stunned after that meeting, and I have never seen him so close to tears in all our years together. I was so sorry for him and I wanted to protect him from those Germans.

I decided to take matters into my own hands, I felt compelled to try to help my husband out of that terrible mess. It was now obvious that he could not carry on with Bremen; they could not treat Dave Watson like that, I would not let them. I telephoned Inge, my only English-speaking link with the club, and pointed out to her that if the club did decide to stop David travelling to Britain for the game against Northern Ireland that they would be in breach of the contract and Dave would then be able to free himself from his obligation to Werder Bremen by declaring the contract broken. Similarly, if they tried to make him pay for the items they had agreed to provide, another clause would be broken. I think the club were taken by surprise by this counter-attack from me – Germans are not used to people questioning authority. I don't know whether my involvement had any effect or not, but at least it made me feel better, and it could not do any harm as things just could not have got any worse than they already were. The whole matter had gotten out of hand, yet the club had the audacity and nerve to say to Dave after fining him and blocking his game for England, that they still wanted him to play for Werder and hoped he would play well. But he had made his mind up that he would never kick another ball for them. Who can blame him?

The club then said that if he did want to return to England for good, that any purchasing club would have to repay every penny they had spent including Dave's transfer fee, his wages, the fines and all the items that they had had to provide for him. All the time we had been at Bremen, Rudi

Assauer had kept a file with every last detail in it and every single bill relating to Dave. There was even one for the cost of fitting a child seat into the car even though the club had been obliged to provide this. (The German clubs are permitted to provide many things for their players that clubs in England cannot.) Not only did they want to recoup the transfer fee but they wanted to double it! On reflection they probably made those stipulations believing they were 'out-pricing' Dave and that no club would then want to buy him, but Rudi had not reckoned on the determination of the English.

Throughout his stay in Germany, David had kept in touch with Lawrie McMenemy, whom Dave had known since his Rotherham days. In fact Southampton had been interested in buying him at the time of his initial transfer from Manchester City, but Dave had made his mind up to go to play in Europe for reasons previously mentioned. Manchester City were still following Dave's progress, but although we would have dearly loved to have returned to Manchester, Malcolm Allison was still there, 'rebuilding' City. Dave flew home to England to prepare for the game against Northern Ireland, and took that opportunity to see Lawrie, discuss contracts and then sign for Southampton. While this was happening, in the German Press, Rudi had said that he had not given Watson permission to go to England or to discuss a transfer to Southampton, that he was still a Werder player and would be severely reprimanded on his return. That was a complete lie, as Lawrie had spoken to Rudi personally, as well as the agent who was negotiating the deal between the two clubs. Of course Dave did sign for Southampton, and he did play for England.

So I was faced once again with the task of transferring all our possessions and furniture back across the North Sea. I was a little sad that our stay in Germany had not been a success for Dave, because the opportunity of living in a foreign country was a great attraction and the possibility of learning to speak fluently another language had greatly appealed to me. My second language was French, but it could hardly be described as fluent. Even though we had only lived there for three months we had already made some good friends amongst the army personnel and had been eagerly welcomed into their close-knit community. The facilities of the sergeants' mess were made available to us, and we had attended several functions there.

One memorable night was the 'Ladies' Night', when all the wives had a mess dinner, while the men were waiters. Most mess dinners are 'men only', so occasionally a ladies' evening was arranged 'to keep the wives quiet'. My parents were staying at the time and my mother and I were not too enthusiastic at the prospect of spending the evening with eighty other women. The evening began rather austerely, but it soon turned into one of the best nights' entertainments I have experienced after all inhibitions had been thrown to the wind following numerous glasses of wine. One of the waiters was threatened with a stripping unless he forfeited a song, and several of the women provided 'off the cuff' entertainment, singing risqué songs and such like. When the time came to finally meet up with our husbands who had been waiting in the bar a band of exuberant and inebriated ladies emerged from the dining-room.

Once again we had to say good-bye to some really good friends. Mike Cole and Sally had helped us on numerous occasions, and we were sorry to leave them behind, but such is the life of a footballer.

I had the task of making in reverse all the arrangements I had carried out three months previously. The same firm of furniture removers were used to export-pack, even though they had not yet been paid by Werder Bremen for our move to Germany, the house had to be put up for sale, and my car had to go too. Fortunately Mike Cole bought that off me, but the house proved to be a problem. Houses are not bought and sold so frequently in Germany as in England, as many people there still do not own their own properties. It was many months before the house was finally disposed of.

Dave was happy at the prospect of playing English soccer once more and was glad to be rid of Rudi Assauer. He was a little sorry that his transfer had not worked out, if only for the other players and the trainer, Wolfgang Weber, with whom Dave had always got on well, but he was looking forward to settling down to some sort of normality again.

Dave:

A fee was agreed between City and Bremen, and my personal terms were sorted out. The good thing about the terms was that we did not have to sell our house in Hale if we did not want to, because I had had the club agree to providing us with a house for two years, rent-free. For tax purposes we did in fact sell our house, but we had not expected to have to purchase another one in Germany. I had arranged that the club would look for suitable houses, so that when we came back from holiday in America we could hopefully just choose one of them. When we did go over they had not done anything about it, and it was left to Penny to set the ball rolling. In the end, because of the time factor, we reluctantly decided to buy our own, which *turned out to be a big mistake. When eventually all the family came over I naturally wanted to fetch them: it is no joke coping with three young children and all the suitcases too. However, the manager, Rudi Assauer, was far from willing to let me go.*

At Werder all the players seemed to be treated the same, even the amateurs. It appeared to me that I had got to the top of my profession only to be treated like an amateur. I found this very hard to take. While playing a game in Stuttgart I must have twisted my knee or received a knock on it, because the next morning it was slightly swollen. I went for treatment, and to my surprise all they did was spread cream on it and massage it in, after which I was told I could train in the afternoon. I knew from experience that when you get fluid on any joint the best thing is to let it settle down. Their methods of treating injuries became another source of friction between me and the club.

Finally, in a game against Munich 1860 I was sent off. It seemed to be the climax of all the problems that had been mounting up. The last straw, I suppose, was being told on the Friday evening before that match that one of the players was criticizing me in the paper. I was very bitter because, apart from the goalkeeper, not one of them had even made a name for himself. What right had that player, I thought, to be attacking me? The result of the sending-off was a long ban – eight weeks – and during that time many more problems arose, as Penny has mentioned.

After the suspension, when the time came for me to play again, my knee was still not right. Even though I had not played for Bremen I had had two England games during my suspension, and I was still forced to train at Bremen, so the knee had been given little chance to recover. To top it all, I got a kick during training on my other knee, so on the Saturday of my 'return' match I could not play. This resulted in my being fined 10,000 DM. After that there seemed to be only one thing left to do: cut our losses and go home, to England. Luckily Southampton came to my rescue, but Rudi Assauer was hardly co-operative. He totted up all the expenses that Werder had incurred involving me, and added them to the transfer fee.

8

Rescued by Saints

Southampton, 1979–82

Lawrie McMenemy had suggested, so that we could all return to England immediately, that we should live in a rented furnished house in Hampshire and put our furniture into store while we looked for a house to buy. This seemed like a good idea, except that the only property available within travelling distance of Southampton was in a small, isolated village called Braishfield, near Romsey, and it was a bungalow which was really too small for our family of five. It only had three bedrooms, so the two older children had to share, while Gemma, still something of an insomniac, had the smallest room to herself. It also meant that we could not have friends and family to stay with us during our spell there, unless they were prepared to rough it.

We had already sent Tina ahead of us to a quarantine kennels in Hampshire. Even though I believe strongly in the control of rabies, I felt sorry for the poor dog having to be imprisoned for six months through no fault of her own, but at least we were able to visit her regularly once each week. On reflection it was a good thing anyway that she was not with us in that small bungalow.

During the two weeks prior to the family returning to England, Dave was permitted to make frequent visits back to Germany after he had played his games for Southampton. His first game, on the Saturday after the Northern Ireland game, was at West Bromwich, where the team lost

4–0, and his debut for the Saints resulted in him sustaining a fractured bone in his face. However, this did not deter him from playing in the next League game at the Dell against Leeds, but once again he was on the losing side, though he was not as despondent as he might normally have been, because he was so pleased to be playing in the Football League again.

There were almost as many forms and regulations to comply with on leaving Germany as there were on entering it, but at least this time David was available some of the time to offer assistance. When the removers arrived to pack up our belongings we had to be careful to make sure that the items we required in Braishfield were not packed to go into store, but despite our meticulous vigilance inevitably some items did find their way to the wrong destination.

When we flew back to England on the evening of 31 October, Halloween Night, having said yet more farewells to new-found friends, we wondered what lay in store for us on this next adventure. Indeed our welcome was rather off-putting. After a very tiring day, during which we had been supervising removals and had travelled some distance to Southampton, we arrived at the bungalow. I remember David saying to me that I was not to expect too much of the bungalow, and generally preparing me for the worst, but when we drove up outside the property I thought he had been exaggerating as it looked quite presentable. It was rather small, admittedly, but even this was better than staying in an hotel for any length of time with the children.

However, when we went inside I cried tears of frustration, anger and tiredness. Apart from being minute, it was absolutely filthy, with dirt and cobwebs hanging in every room and even a dirty old commode in the lounge. There was no bed linen, and we had not brought any with us on the plane. We had put some aside for the removers to bring, but that would not arrive for another two days. We thought of going to Lawrie for help, as he lived in the same village, but it was eleven o'clock at night and too late to bother him.

I have always had a terrible phobia about spiders, and the thought of having to spend a night under the same roof as all those creatures made me cringe. Dave tried his best to clear up the rooms, as the children were dropping from exhaustion and desperately in need of a good night's sleep. A cot which had been left for Gemma but was still dismantled was hastily assembled, and as I had been able to pack her cot quilt she at least could be bedded. I cannot quite remember how, but we managed to clear the other bedrooms into some sort of order and slept with makeshift bedding over us all.

The morning light indicated that the bungalow was even filthier than we had first thought, and it looked as though it had not been inhabited for quite some time. Fortunately Mrs McMenemy came to our rescue with fresh clean linen to tide us over until ours arrived. She told us that after she had seen the bungalow the previous day, when she kindly bought a few provisions and checked the central heating for us, so that at least we would have a warm welcome, she had mentioned to Lawrie that it was not very clean. Just how filthy the place was can be imagined when I say that industrial cleaners had to be employed to make the place clean again.

Dave had only one day to help sort things out before he was off on his travels once again. On the Friday the team went up to Manchester, as they were playing against Manchester United on the Saturday. That Friday night I had little sleep as the lights fused and I had not yet had time to acquaint myself with the house, so I did not know where the fuse-box was or where any candles could be found. The children still liked to have a light on at night, and as there were no street lamps in Braishfield it was pitch black.

Unfortunately David did not play, and had to be brought home by our friend Tom Whittaker, as he had been taken ill during the Friday night with what appeared to be food poisoning.

The furniture van arrived on the Saturday to drop off all our clothes and a few other pieces of furniture that we had wanted at the bungalow. These they just dumped and left for me to unpack. Lugging heavy boxes around, while simultaneously coping with a young family and a very sick husband, I felt exasperated and depressed and wondered why we seemed to be having so much turmoil in our lives. The past six months had been hell for us as a family – not really knowing where we were going to be in a few months' time and never being allowed to lay down roots. In my twisted logic I blamed Malcolm Allison for all our bad fortune, for there was no doubt in my mind that, had he not returned to Manchester City, we would have still been there amongst our friends and living a life we all enjoyed.

The bout of self-pity over, I attacked the task in hand to try to make some sort of order in which we could live. I could not help cursing David, though, for choosing that moment in time to contract food poisoning, and I think my comforting bedside manner probably deserted me then! However, he returned to play the following Saturday against Nottingham Forest at the Dell, when the home team convincingly won 4–1 and – best news of all – Dave scored his first goal for Southampton. I had once again been fortunate in that I had been able to find a babysitter immediately, so I was able to watch that game.

Roger and Heather were then settled into yet another school, in Romsey, but although the staff there were understanding and sympathetic, Heather found it difficult to settle, as she knew it was probably only another temporary measure until we found a house of our own. Of all the children, she was most affected by the confusion of the previous few months and, always a very shy child, she withdrew completely into her shell and her school work during that time suffered greatly. Roger had always been more resilient, and the constant change of schools did not seem to trouble him – or at least we were never aware of any problems. Gemma was still Gemma, the active, demanding lovable villain of the family, and all the changes came at a bad time for her in that we were in the process of trying, unsuccessfully, to nappy-train her.

How I cursed football during those months! My appetite for the game certainly diminished somewhat, as if I were blaming football for causing all the enforced changes in our lives. Even now I do not think I am so passionate about the game as I was previously, and I find my mind wandering at some matches. I cannot say for sure, but perhaps after fourteen years I now sense that our personal involvement in the game will soon be over, and I may be subconsciously reacting in this way to cushion the blow when the axe finally falls on Dave's career.

When we first moved into the rented place we thought that the four or five months we were due to be living there would be ample time to search for a new home for us to purchase. In reality it became a desperate rush towards the end, as there were just no suitable properties on the market, and we were finally forced into buying a house which, under normal circumstances, we would probably not have considered. Curiously, though, it turned out to be the most attractive and convenient house we had ever had during our marriage. The reason we were forced into a hasty decision was that the owners of the bungalow, who had been living abroad, decided to return home, and we had to vacate the property for their arrival in the spring.

Dave immediately settled into his new footballing environment, where there were plenty of familiar faces. There was

Mike Channon, who had returned to Southampton from Manchester City, and Alan Ball, whom Dave knew from Bally's England days, and several other players with whom he had become acquainted over the years in soccer. He did have to adapt in some ways on joining a small club – after all his last English club had been one of the largest in the country – but the very fact that the ground itself is so tiny, with such a small crowd capacity, in itself creates a unique, close atmosphere. All the same, the football club and Southampton itself would benefit greatly from a new ground if the planners ever have the foresight to realize this.

Dave was surprised when Lawrie secured the signature of Kevin Keegan, because he had been away with Kevin the previous week for an England session. At no time was anything mentioned to Dave, even though negotiations must have been well under way. He felt very excluded, insignificant and stupid when, without prior knowledge, Kevin turned up in Southampton a few days later. Dave had been accustomed at City, along with all the other senior professionals and not just because he was captain, to being kept informed of significant changes within the club.

Kevin's signing did initially create pandemonium at the club, and for a time the other players appeared to have to take a back seat. No lasting animosity was caused, but during all the confusion and euphoria one of the players was heard to remark, 'We all know who will win next season's player of the year.' It was not that the players were jealous of Kevin – just a little disgruntled at the sudden change in the running of things. Soon everything was back in perspective and began to tick along nicely once more.

One game David was looking forward to playing was against Manchester City at the Dell. Malcolm Allison was still the manager for the opposition, and both Mike Channon and Dave desired revenge on the football pitch. During the match Dave was outstanding, and Southampton beat City 4–1.

The penultimate Southampton goal was brilliantly taken by Dave, but in the process of heading the ball he was in a collision with Joe Corrigan, City's giant goalkeeper, who appeared to mis-punch the ball and instead made contact with Dave's head. Dave fell heavily to the ground and was unconscious for several anxious moments. By some medical mix-up between the physiotherapist and trainer who had both run on to the pitch to revive him, Dave was allowed to continue playing when he was severely concussed.

Because of the position he plays and the constant heading of the ball with such great power, and because of the many head injuries – some eight or nine of them – he has sustained in the course of his career, his head must fast be reaching a condition similar to a boxer's. All it needed was for him to head another ball while in a concussed state, and I dread to think what might have happened. Fortunately the collision occurred near the end of the match and he was not called on to head the ball. In actual fact he was running around without a clue where he was, unaware that he had scored and after the final whistle had to be shown where the dressing-rooms were.

When I was called down to the treatment room I realized that Dave must have still been confused, as indeed he was, but I did not realize the full extent of his condition until I was driving him home. He could not remember his way home, he could only vaguely remember the bungalow, he had forgotten all about Christmas some six weeks before, and he kept repeating the same questions over and over again.

This went on for several hours until Lawrie called to see

how he was and we decided that Dave was in no fit state to be at home, so he was admitted to the Southampton General Hospital. There – believe it or not – even during his admission a nurse, who should have known better, pestered him for his autograph. (Sue George once told me that when Charlie was admitted as an emergency after accidentally chopping off his fingers with the lawn mower, the nurses at the hospital in Winchester, where he went, were even bothering him to sign autographs. Of course he was in no fit state to – after all, half his hand was missing!)

After a stay in hospital Dave was rested and at least ceased the repeated questioning that had worried me so much, but he still could remember little of the proceedings on that Saturday. Even now, although most of his amnesia has gone, four or five hours are still missing in his memory. He slept almost continuously for five days: Dave normally hates staying in bed for any length of time, so his mind must have needed that rest to recuperate. Once again my nursing experience led me to imagine that all the complications that *could* occur in such cases would happen to Dave, and I had visions of him collapsing at some future date with a blood clot or some such thing. My over-active imagination again! Nevertheless I was extremely worried, and I just hope that nothing like that ever happens to him again. The consultant he saw had been at the game himself, and he was amazed at the decision to allow Dave to continue playing; he said that it was indeed a bad case of concussion.

The saddest thing is that Dave still has no memory of scoring the goal. Fortunately the television cameras were there, and when the match was shown on the television that night I was able to video-record it, so he has at least been able to see it, but the sweetness of the revenge from that goal will probably always elude him. A few lessons were learned by the club, however, and Lawrie made certain that in future concussed players would be properly diagnosed and instantly taken out of the game for immediate hospitalization.

Once we had moved into our new home in Southampton and the children had settled, yet again, in their new schools and Tina was released from quarantine, the whole family began to establish itself in its new surroundings. Dave was fortunate to become involved in another business venture in shipping, and at long last normality returned.

During this period, the summer of 1980, the England team had qualified for the finals of the European Championships, which were held in Italy. I had independently booked to go to Italy with a girlfriend, Sue Young, as this was to be the highlight of Dave's career and I had every intention of sharing it with him. Of course the wives were not automatically sent to Italy, though I know some people outside football imagine they always are. Those of us who did make our way, did so entirely of our own accord. Another friend was looking after the children for me, so I could go to Italy to have a relaxing holiday.

The experiences we encountered there were anything but relaxing, and when I was asked later if I enjoyed my holiday all I could say was that it was 'different'. The animosity shown to the English was unbelievable. England were drawn to play in the same group as the favourites and host nation, and the Italians mistakenly assumed that the English would be their nearest rivals. Intimidation and aggravation was commonplace throughout our stay there, and if I had not seen with my own eyes some of the things that the police allowed to go on, I would not have believed them. The night we arrived on the Italian Riviera, a few English boys were chased by several young Italians, and in the ensuing fight one of the English boys was pushed through a plate glass window in our hotel. When the police arrived the Italians were allowed to go scot-free, but the poor English lads were taken to prison and they had to pay for the damaged window (which was no doubt insured anyway).

My friend and I, along with my parents who had also made the trip to Italy, attended that first eventful game in Turin against the Belgians. Before the game, around the stadium the English lads were in high spirits singing songs and chanting slogans. The Belgians, though there were only a few of them, entered into the spirit too and were singing their own songs, mainly in English. There was no trouble at all between the two factions. However, as the football fans entered the stadium we were all subjected to a security search, and many of the English boys' treasured banners, which had been lovingly made to bring for these championships, had the poles taken out of them and these were then thrown onto a pile. The lads were told to collect them on their way out, but of course that proved impractical and impossible.

The night before the game I was told that the police raided camp-sites in the area. The English contingent were all fast asleep in their sleeping bags to be abruptly woken by zealous young policemen brandishing truncheons. There were several such incidents by all accounts, and the Italians seem to have done everything possible to provoke the English.

One such atrocious incident which I witnessed myself occurred after the final whistle. We were all making our way round the outside of the stadium – hordes of despondent English – when to my complete and utter astonishment a young Italian went up to a very respectable, tall, unobtrusive young Englishman who was walking along on his own, and started repeatedly prodding the man. The English fellow held both his hands up in a surrender pose, but the Italian continued prodding, intimidating and trying to provoke this man into retaliation. I have nothing but praise for that young man, who must have walked a hundred yards with this going on. All it needed was for him to lose control and render a blow, and the whole area would have been under tear-gas, for at the top of the road was an armoured car (at a football match!) with policemen and soldiers pointing their weapons towards us. To all intents and purposes it looked like a set-up job. The trouble in the stadium was also instigated by the planted Italian agitators who had been allowed to stand and chant abuse at the English in what should have been our enclosure.

I am usually the first person to condemn football hooliganism, but what I saw happen forces even me to commiserate with the so-called 'trouble-makers' amongst the English crowd. The real trouble-makers, the Italians, were again allowed to escape scot-free. To say that the Italian police over-reacted would be putting it mildly. The trouble was initially confined to one corner, and I would say it involved at the most twelve people. Any police force worth its salt should be able to deal with that sort of problem without causing havoc. Indeed the problem seemed to have been settled, and many of the other supporters in that enclosure had sat down to concentrate on what they had paid so much to come and see, when rushing up the stairs emerged ferocious immature Italian police waving their huge truncheons and hitting at random completely innocent people. It was a disgrace, and I am only thankful that Dave had seen where I was sitting before the kick-off, so that he knew I was relatively safe.

The police then started firing, and what the poor English defence must have thought – they had their backs to all this – I dread to imagine. After a split second, when the gas started floating around, we suddenly realized, though we could hardly believe it, that they had fired tear-gas. So competently too! One can had been shot completely out of the football stadium, another had hit the scoreboard and broken it, and another was so near the pitch that the game had to be stopped for a while as the players themselves were affected by the gas. That was the first time I had heard of a football game being stopped because of tear-gas.

The next game against Italy was one game I reluctantly stayed and watched on the television. Since the Belgium game the English had been subjected to more abuse and ridicule, and on every street corner there seemed to be groups of young Italians. The coaches that had been booked to take our party to the game were withdrawn at the last minute and arrangements were quickly made for a special train, but the station was some distance from the football ground and no buses would take the English supporters into Turin. Every effort was made to try to force the supporters to miss the game, but thankfully most of the English were undaunted and in fact were even more determined to cheer on their team.

Nevertheless, it was not recommended that women went, so reluctantly my mother, my friend Sue, Kevin Keegan's sister-in-law Jill, and a couple of other English women crowded round the hotel television instead. I was sad that I had been forced to miss this game, as it was one I had particularly looked forward to, but Dave had intimated that he did not want me to go and that he would be happier knowing I was safe.

Even when the players themselves went out to do some shopping or have a walk around, they were given no protection and were subjected to hostility. One day Stevie Coppell and Dave went out but were soon forced to retreat to the hotel by intimidating young Italians on their mopeds who hurled abuse at them. The Italians really have no idea about running such an important competition. A couple of the players, including Dave, had quite a bit of money stolen from their hotel bedrooms – such was their security. These incidents went on all through our trip, and many hotels refused to take English people – even some hotels which had been booked well in advance and where deposits had been paid. I was naturally sorry that the England team had not achieved the success hoped for, but I was extremely glad to get away from Italy and I will not be in too much of a hurry to return.

Immediately after our return from Italy, I was admitted to hospital for a long overdue operation to help cure problems relating to my prolapsed womb. I had been trying for two years to fit the operation in between football seasons – in order to create the minimum of disorder at home – and finally I was able to achieve this, though the numerous pre-season tours that Lawrie had arranged did prove occasionally troublesome.

The main problem was that after such an operation the patient is not allowed to lift heavy objects for a recommended three months. This is a difficult task, when you have a young family, so relations rallied round to ensure my full recovery, and of course Dave was marvellous too during that period. Had I been left unsupervised there is little doubt that I would have been tempted to do something I should not have done, so the watchful eyes were not only much appreciated but necessary. It was during the long convalescence following that operation that I first thought of writing this book to help ease the tremendous boredom I was suffering.

Having learned through experience, I now carefully sift through any invitations to functions which include me. So often a celebrity's wife (or husband) can be left in the background like a 'spare part' at social gatherings, and on occasions can even be treated quite rudely. There are, thankfully, some exceptions, where I have been treated with hospitality, notably the functions we attend after international matches at Wembley organized by Tim Atkin, who has been a friend of Dave's for years, and Peter Thomas. These are very friendly, informal occasions where we can both relax.

Over the years I have had the opportunity to meet numerous celebrities, outside of the football circle, but as name-dropping is not an attribute I admire in others I will resist the temptation to do the same. However, no book about Dave or me would be complete without mentioning one group of people who have become an integral part of our lives since we first had the good fortune to meet them. Rick Parfitt and Francis Rossi are not only members of Status Quo rock band but are also very good friends of ours. An avid amateur musician and songwriter, Dave's love of the Quo's music stems from many years previously when I confess that my interest was still to be developed. However, following a live concert in Sunderland in 1973 my curiosity was aroused and I too became a 'fan', though I hasten to add never quite on the same scale as David.

Dave never actually met the band until December 1977, when they were playing at the Apollo, Manchester. I had just had Gemma, so I was not fit to attend, but Dave went, and took along – in the hope of 'converting' them – Willie Donachie and Kenny Clements. Andy Peebles, who was still a DJ with the local radio, Radio Piccadilly, arranged with the help of Bob Young, who was Quo's road manager at the time, for the players to visit the group back-stage before the performance.

Bob Young was in the future to become one of Dave's closest friends, and it was his wife Sue who went to Italy with me for the European Championships. Our only regret is that we do not live nearer to their home in Surrey, because the four of us get on so well together. Corny as it may sound, there was an immediate bond between Quo and Dave. Most of the band were keen football fans, none more so than Rick, who was not a bad footballer himself. Over the years our friendship has developed and we are now very honoured to be incorporated in the close-knit 'family' of Quo, an inclusion that pleases us more than we can say.

In March 1978 the band flew us over, as their guests, to Zurich, where we saw them perform during their European tour of that year. Later the same year we went to stay with the group for a couple of days in Amsterdam, where they were recording an album. They in turn would watch Dave play in England games and occasionally in club games for Manchester City and subsequently Southampton.

We are fortunate in that now we do live a little nearer to Rick and Marietta Parfitt, and consequently we see more of them. It would be difficult to find a more caring and devoted mother than Marietta, Rick's German-born wife. However, accidents can happen, even in the most loving environment. As well as their son Richard, who is six, they also had a gorgeous little girl, just a few months younger than Gemma, called Heidi. We first saw her when she was only five weeks old, and I fondly cherish the memory of the moment when I fed and changed her at such a tender age.

Throughout our time in Southampton we would visit the Parfitts at home for the day, usually on a Sunday – Dave's only day off – and the children would enjoy themselves playing together in Rick's large house or in the nine-acre grounds. During our visits I can honestly say that I never heard Heidi cry; she was such a lovable, angelic child who always seemed to have a smile on her pretty little face. Marietta had always strived to give the children a normal home life, something which can be difficult to achieve in the pop business, and there is no doubt that Heidi was a credit to her mother.

One tragic Sunday, a day on which we had intended to visit them but decided against it as Gemma was still infectious with chicken pox, for some unaccountable reason, Heidi decided to go to the swimming pool which is situated some distance from their house. One moment she was in the kitchen talking to her mummy, who was preparing the Sunday lunch, and saying that she was going to find daddy who was playing in another part of the house with Richard, and the next moment she had drowned.

Eventually no obstacle can deter an inquisitive determined mind, and even though Heidi knew she should not go near the pool and had never tried to do so before, that particular moment in time, fate decided that she should satisfy her curiosity. Later that evening, as soon as we had heard the terrible news, we went to their home to try to help our grieving friends. I do not know whether we were really of much assistance – I think possibly we were, as both Rick and Marietta have indicated as much to us – but at least we felt that we had to try to help our friends through that ordeal.

Since then, possibly due to the fact that we were with them when they were at their most vulnerable and tried to offer them practical help, our friendship has taken on a new and deeper meaning. A lot of little good things seem to be coming out of the tragedy of Heidi's death. I know that when I feel depressed about things which are really trivial matters, thinking of Heidi soon puts life back into perspective. Her funeral was the most moving event I have ever attended, and my admiration goes out to Rick and Marietta for the way in which they are trying so hard to carry on a normal life under such dreadful circumstances. I truly hope our friendship will continue for many years.

Even Francis Rossi, always the most reserved of the band and something of a hermit, visits the Dell with his son Nicholas and has become a fervent football supporter, or should I say 'Dave Watson supporter'. The friendship of all the band is something that probably would never have happened without football.

15 October 1980 saw England losing 2–1 against a very skilful and underestimated Rumanian side away and it was a game that Dave soon wished he had not played in. Undoubtedly he had not played as well as in his normal England performances, but there were many others who, on the day, did not perform to their maximum ability. However, he soon became the 'whipping boy' of some of the English Press. We live in a curious country in that when people reach the height of their professions our national Press is all too eager to knock them off the top and to try to replace them by other persons they personally have championed. If Ron Greenwood listened to every suggestion that the media make in the hope of influencing his judgement of who and who not to play, England would have a very unsettled side indeed.

This trial by the reporters does not just apply to football but to many professions in the arts. After fifty-six performances for his country, after emerging as one of the few successful players in the European Championships in Italy only four months previously, overnight David became 'too old for the job'. Of course a player does not just suddenly become too old; even in the case of a rapid decline it is only fair to reserve judgement for several games. The new severe criticism of David was something he had never had to encounter before during his years in the game. It was enough for him to be disappointed with his own performance without the retribution that followed in the newspapers. Inevitably Dave then started to have doubts himself about his future career with England, but Ron Greenwood soon dispelled them for him.

His age had worried him a little, but many people lose

sight of the fact that he entered League football so late and therefore has three or four years on most professionals in that demanding life. His pace has eased a little, but with his particular gait it often looks as though he is running much slower than he actually is. Even in his early days, when people like Tommy Docherty were prompted to say how fast Dave was, he had looked much slower than he was. Unfortunately, some of the footballing crowd in Southampton are affected by what they read in the Press, and it seemed that his following performances were scrutinized as though under magnifying glasses. This attitude only unnerved Dave and made things worse for him. Oh for a footballing crowd like Sunderland's, where undoubtedly they would have got behind him and supported him in the true meaning of the word! There is not a professional in the Football League who has not at some time during his career gone through a bad patch, and so far Dave had escaped this experience. I remember Southampton 'supporters' putting Alan Ball through the same trauma when we had first come to the south coast. Of course the only place Dave could prove he was not 'over the hill' was on the football park, and when his confidence returned and the whole team started playing well again, his critics were duly silenced.

He was to receive his greatest honour in the spring of 1981, when on 29 April he was asked to captain England in a World Cup qualifying match against Rumania. It was a very proud Dave who led the team out on to the Wembley turf that night, and even though the team did not win Dave had a magnificent game. This was most surprising, as only the day before he had been very doubtful about playing at all, on account of an injured knee. However, the promise of the England captaincy was just the incentive he needed to overcome the psychological doubt. I too was bursting with pride and was delighted when he went on to captain

England on two more occasions. He has kept his captain's arm-bands, which are displayed in a prominent position in his trophy cabinet.

Dave:

I had known Lawrie McMenemy for most of my footballing career, so he was no stranger; and I also knew one of the players, Mick Channon, who had returned to Southampton from Manchester City not long before I arrived. I settled in quite well and had a reasonable first season, keeping my place in the England team. As part of the England squad I went to Italy for the European Championships. It was a big disappointment for all concerned, because a lot more was expected of us and by us.

The following season started very well for the Saints, who only lost one game in their first eight. Then, after an England game in Rumania, which we lost, I was criticized very strongly by some of the national Press, even though the goals scored against us were not my fault in any way. Throughout my career it has seemed that some of the Press have never taken to me and have seized every opportunity to criticize me. Well, I have been in the international set-up since October 1973 – and the only time I have not was through my back injury – so somebody must be wrong, and I like to think it is not the successive England managers.

A dream came true when I first met Status Quo, and since then I have become good friends with, initially, Bob Young, then Rick Parfitt and later Francis Rossi. The rock business is one that I like a lot and would love to be part of it in some way. I have written several songs and have even made a demo-tape with the help of Francis, but as yet nothing has materialized.

The tragic accident that happened to Rick's daughter, Heidi, meant that for the first time I was close to someone in death, and it made me feel very inadequate. Penny wrote a letter of sympathy to Rick and Marietta, and they were so moved by it that they planned to frame it for all to see. That is a measure of Penny! I recall, at the funeral, Rick's mother saying that the letter had been a great help to them all and that it was wonderful that Penny could write like that.

Penny:

Where the next step may take us when, sooner or later, Dave has finished playing for Southampton, who can say? Fortunately I have been able to look upon every new experience I have encountered during my years of marriage as an adventure, and no one can say that so far my life has been dull. One possibility of the future is that the time will then be ripe for Dave to go to North America and take on a fresh new challenge. The Americans have undoubtedly produced a novel concept in soccer, in many ways new and different to our own, and although initially many people in Britain, including myself and Dave, scoffed at the American approach to football, those same people now have to admit that things seem to be working extremely well across the Atlantic.

When Dave finally hangs up his boots, his business interests will, hopefully, have taken off and be able to contribute to maintaining our present standard of living. Whatever transpires I know that I will be right there with him, the other side of the Watson team, supporting and urging him on as I have always done in the past. He always said that he did not wish to remain in football once his playing days are finished but his attitude towards this, as he matures, has mellowed and if the right offer came along he might be tempted, though I think for the future his heart lies in the business world. I strongly believe that whatever Dave does he will strive to be successful at and hopefully achieve his next ambition in life which is to be a prosperous businessman. I certainly hope so, because, even if I say so myself – and I know I'm biased – he is a hell of a nice lad!

Some of the friends we have made and the standard of living we now have might never have been achieved without soccer. So taking everything into account I must admit that, despite the many pitfalls and disadvantages, football has been good to me and my family but I am looking forward to being able one day in the future, to do those things that 'normal' families take for granted but which football sometimes prohibits. But don't write Dave Watson off yet, there is still a lot left in the 'old' man, and he will be the first to know, with a little help from me, when the time is right to pack it in.